CONTENTS | SYSTEMIC RISK

LIMN NUMBER ONE
edited by Stephen J. Collier
Christopher M. Kelty and Andrew Lakoff

"What are the political implications of a focus among government officials and technical experts on systemic risk?"

Preface

ISSUE ONE | **SYSTEMIC RISK**

▶ **THIS ISSUE OF** LIMN examines the concept of systemic risk. Systemic risk has become a central topic of expert discussion and political debate amidst the financial crisis that began in 2008, but it also has resonances across many other domains in which catastrophic threats loom—including internet security, supply chain management, catastrophe insurance, and critical infrastructure protection. Following the broad orientations of the magazine, we have not tried to present a comprehensive exposition of the history and present uses of systemic risk. Instead, we have invited scholars to contribute genealogical and conceptual framings that can inform critical inquiry into this increasingly important concept. The result is not a traditional collection of academic articles but rather a set of brief, preliminary reflections, prepared on short notice, that address a common set of questions:

What are the contemporary domains in which the concept of systemic risk is most relevant, and what are the interconnections among these domains?

What historical points of reference might help render contemporary discussions of systemic risk intelligible, and provide genealogical framings for a critical analysis of systemic risk?

What are the political implications of a focus among government officials and technical experts on systemic risk?

As the contributions from Douglas Holmes, Onur Ozgöde and Grahame Thompson indicate, the concept of systemic risk has acquired a specific meaning in recent debates among economists and policy-makers about financial regulatory reform. Deregulation initiatives during the 1990s were based on the assumption that the risk of large-scale financial collapse could be mitigated by allowing individual firms to manage risks on their own portfolios. The recent financial crisis, however, shifted attention to risks that stem from the exposure of entire asset classes to "catastrophic" events—such as the exposure of mortgage-backed securities to a downturn in the US housing market—and to financial instruments—such as collateralized debt obligations—that concentrate rather than spread such risk. Reformers thus used the concept of systemic risk to analyze the vulnerabilities created by the accumulation of risk at critical points in the financial system, placing a particular accent on events that cause the co-variation of individual risks.[1]

The challenge posed by the co-variation of risks is also apparent in the domain of catastrophe insurance. Traditional models of insurantial risk assessment focus on loss-causing events (sickness, workplace injury, or death, for example) that are distributed over a population. Traditional insurance works because such individual risks do not co-vary. Life insurance, for example, is built on the proposition that the death of one policyholder in an insurance pool does not significantly change the risk of death of other policy-holders, and it is thus possible to "spread" individual risks across a population. Catastrophe insurance, which has become increasingly important in the last two decades as insurance companies have dealt with "superdisasters" such as 9/11 and the hurricanes of the early 1990s, presents a different problem. For an insurer in south Florida, a hurricane that caused losses for one insured property would also cause losses for other policyholders in its portfolio. In other words, in contrast to the usual assumption of insurance, losses from a catastrophe are likely to display high levels of co-variation. Here, too, systemic risk is something more than an aggregation of individual risks. It is, rather, an emergent property of the insurance system itself.

These discussions of systemic risk in finance and insurance point to a more general feature of the contemporary problematization of risk. Insurance and financial systems are crucial to modern economies as mechanisms of security (in the case of insurance) and of economic growth (in the case of finance). But the very condition of their success in performing these functions—the ability of insurance to spread risk over populations, the ability of the financial system to allocate capital over a broad range of economic activities—also produces new vulnerabilities that grow and ramify as systems become increasing interconnected and complex. Here, the concept of systemic risk converges with the logic of what Ulrich Beck has called "modernization risk." For Beck, modernization risks—such as mass casualty terrorism, ecological crises, and global financial meltdowns—are generated by the success of modernization processes. In other words, they are a product of the very systems—of finance, of insurance, of transportation and communication, of industrial production—that provide for the health and well-being of populations. This connection was made explicit in a 2003 OECD study, analyzed here by Myriam Dunn, which focused on risks that affect not only individuals but also "the systems on which society depends": "Health services, transport, energy, food and water supplies, information and telecommunications are all examples of sectors with vital systems that can be severely damaged by a single catastrophic chain of events."

Seen in this way, it quickly becomes apparent that the problem of systemic risk is by no means new; indeed, it has consistently accompanied modernization processes over the last century. Timothy Mitchell (2009) has shown that the emergence of complex, integrated industrial systems created vulnerabilities such as the "choke-points" that were exploited by strikers and saboteurs in the early 20th century.[2] In our contribution on domestic preparedness for nuclear war we describe how military planners envisioned the industrial, energy, and transportation systems that were necessary for the conduct of modern warfare as simultaneously sources of vulnerability that could be targeted by an enemy. And as Deborah Cowen observes in her contribution here, the logistics systems that spread from the military to private business after World War II—making industrial supply chains vastly more efficient—also made the same businesses more vulnerable to disruption. New infrastructures have extended the logic of systemic risk into new domains, as in the case of digital information infrastructure—analyzed here by Christopher Kelty—which is a critical area for contemporary discussions of systemic risk. As Myriam Dunn documents, the concern with government information systems initially gave rise to the par-

adigm of Critical Infrastructure Protection in the United States, which was later extended to a broad range of vulnerable systems, from finance, to transportation, to health.

The juxtaposition here of contributions concerning disparate domains brings some surprising connections to light. For example, we see the common origins of certain approaches to envisioning systems at risk and to mitigating their vulnerability. Some techniques come from the sub-disciplines of operations research and systems analysis, as Martha Poon and Deborah Cowen demonstrate; others come from ecology and system dynamics, as we see in contributions from Benjamin Sims and Brian Lindseth. A notable feature of the present conjuncture is a very active process of borrowing, in which experts in one domain—finance or critical infrastructure protection, for example—adapt techniques that have developed in other domains for other purposes. As expertise in the mitigation of systemic risk proliferates, then, new assemblages are emerging that recombine disparate techniques and draw together disparate histories of techno-scientific and governmental practice.

STEPHEN J. COLLIER
ANDREW LAKOFF
JANUARY 2011

---

1 The term "co-variation" indicates the tendency of all the assets in a given class, or multiple asset classes, to respond in the same way to a given event.

2 The term "choke point" refers to any bottleneck in a production process whose disruption would severely reduce output.

Systemic Risk and the Government of Crisis

Various experts analyzing the 2008-10 financial crisis have relied on the concept of "systemic risk" as an explanation. In a widely cited 2003 article, George Kaufman and Kenneth Scott defined systemic risk as the "the risk or probability of breakdowns in an entire system, as opposed to breakdowns in individual parts or components, and is evidenced by co-movements (correlation) among most or all the parts." But the centrality of the problem of systemic risk is not limited to the domain of finance. The National Academy of Science convened a high profile meeting in 2006 to discuss the relation between ecological concepts of catastrophic risk in interdependent systems and systemic risk in finance. In looking at other domains—energy, information, health—one finds similar modes of thinking among experts about both problems and potential solutions.

WHAT IS SYSTEMIC RISK? SOME KEY MOMENTS

  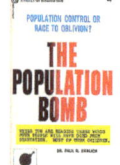  

	1930's STRATEGIC BOMBING	1952 H-BOMB TESTS	1968 THE POPULATION BOMB	1973 ENERGY CRISIS	1978-1983 LATIN AMERICAN DEBT CRISIS	1988 MORIS WORM
	During WWI, Germany used Zeppelins to drop bombs on England, Russia, and France. By the end of WWI and in the years leading up to WWII, Germany and England developed a theory that mass long-range bombing, could potentially result in sufficient loss of morale to make the enemy surrender.	On November 1, 1952, the United States conducted its first hydrogen bomb test, code-named *Mike*, as a part of operation *Ivy*. Mike was part of a series of nuclear tests which marked the dawn of thermonuclear missile age and the beginning of programs of total preparedness and national survival.	The American biologist Paul R. Ehrlich wrote *The Population Bomb*, which sold over 2 million copies, and influenced public policy in the years to come. Population predictions and world-systems modelling adapted models of defence mobilization and disaster planning into the domains of social policy.	The 1973 oil crisis began with the oil embargo in response to the U.S. decision to re-supply the Israeli military during the Yom Kippur war; it lasted until March 1974. It was the first "systemic" crisis in oil markets and led to the effective globalization of oil markets.	The Latin American debt crises of 1978-1983 represent the first instance of the use of the term "Systemic Risk" by William Cline of the Peterson Institute. The debt crisis raised issues of "external shocks" and the question of how insolvency or bankruptcy could be propagated across nations and into the increasingly global economy.	The Morris worm was the first widespread internet worm. It temporarily crippled the Internet and caused major media interest in the problem of the system-wide risks of computer hacking in networked environments.
Key technical or political responses:	Critical target mapping. Stockpiling, redundancy.	Programs for total preparedness, national survival.	World systems theory, computer modeling of crises.	Fuel efficiency standards; national maximum speed limit.	Structural adjustment.	Computer fraud legislation and emergency response teams.
Conceptual connections:	The translation of catastrophe modeling from defense mobilization to natural disasters in the mid-1960s.			The migration of the norm of "resilience" from ecology to systems engineering in response to electrical grid breakdowns in the 1970s.		
Related articles in this Issue:	Collier and Lakoff p. 22	Collier and Lakoff, p. 22	Lindseth, p. 34		Ozgöde p. 27	Kelty, p. 17 Cavelty, p. 12

Problematizing systemic risk reveals at least the following elements:

1 Interdependency Contemporary society depends on complex, interdependent systems—energy grids, information networks, financial systems, and mechanisms of industrial production.

2 Cascading Failures Disruptions of these systems can have cascading effects that lead to systemic collapse.

3 Resilience Proposals for regulatory intervention focus on the notion of "resilience" to perturbations in the system.

1998-2000
Y2K "MILLENIUM BUG" The "Year 2000" bug captured popular attention and highlighted the possible systemic collapse created by engineering decisions taken decades earlier. Before 9/11 it gave momentum to "critical infrastructure planning" projects and proposals.

2000-2001
ENRON AND THE CALIFORNIA ENERGY CRISIS Enron's financial shenanigans combined with the deregulation of energy markets created rolling blackouts in California. The event clearly ensnared consumers in the effects of systemic and infrastructural decisions.

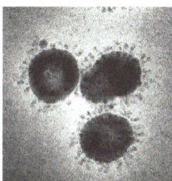

2001
9/11 ATTACKS 9/11 gave enormous momentum to preparedness planning programs, critical infrastructure protection and the exploration of alternative forms of risk and planning, including especially scenario planning.

2002-2003
SARS OUTBREAK A *Severe Acute Respiratory Syndrome* outbreak confirmed fears of emerging diseases and their rapid spread through globally interconnected systems. The near pandemic brought attention to systemic challenges of monitoring, containment and response.

2005
HURRICANE KATRINA The worst natural disaster in recent memory highlighted failures in emergency management, government response, infrastructure maintenance and public trust.

2010
DEEP WATER HORIZON OIL SPILL The out-of-control oil spill in the Gulf of Mexico turned into an engineering drama as BP tried technique after technique to cap the well and stop the flow. It highlighted the absense of expertise concerning deep-water drilling safety.

2008-?
CURRENT FINANCIAL CRISIS A now canonical example of the effect of systemic collapse that combined poor lending decisions in the mortgage market, poorly or unregulated financial engineering, and ineffective oversight by ratings agencies.

| Massive reprogramming efforts aimed at stemming collapse. | Sarbanes-Oxley, energy re-regulation. | Critical infrastructure preparedness; scenario exercises. | Disease early warning systems. Scenario exercises. | | | |

Post 9/11, the generalization of "critical infrastructure protection" from computer network vulnerabilities to a more generic method of assessing infrastructural vulnerability to a terrorist attack.

The adaptation of scenario-based exercises from the military to public health preparedness in the early 2000s, in the wake of SARS and in anticipation of H5N1.

RESILIENCE AND HOMELAND SECURITY
PATRIOTISM, ANXIETY, AND COMPLEX SYSTEM DYNAMICS

BY BENJAMIN SIMS

KATRINA AFTERMATH
A U.S. Army High Mobility Multipurpose Wheeled Vehicle traverses through floodwater surrounding the Superdome in New Orleans, Louisiana, September 2005.

IN THE REALM of U.S. homeland security, the word of the day seems to be "resilience." As a sociologist working in this area, I encounter the term more and more frequently, in a variety of contexts. More publicly, Secretary of Homeland Security Jeannette Napolitano has frequently spoken about her department's efforts to "strengthen the resilience of … infrastructure, computer networks, and of … communities and citizens" (Napolitano, 2010). Resilience is also prominently mentioned in recent Homeland Security policy documents, including the 2010 Quadrennial Homeland Security Review, which lists "Ensuring Resilience to Disasters" as one of five core "Homeland Security Missions" (Dept. of Homeland Security, 2010), and the 2009 National Infrastructure Protection Plan (NIPP), which now emphasizes the dual goals of "protection and resilience" (Dept. of Homeland Security, 2010). The Department of Homeland Security (DHS) sponsors conferences of its grantees in the academic community under the rubric of "Science and Technology for Intelligent Resilience." Resilience is a broad concept as it is used in the homeland security realm—it can refer to the technological nuts and bolts of infrastructure, as well as the more general character of a community, region, or nation. Though it is too soon to say for certain, the term may be on its way to encompassing or displacing more established terms like "protection" and "vulnerability."

The concept of resilience, as it is currently used, has a surprisingly interdisciplinary history. Engineers have long used resilience to refer to the ability of materials to spring back to their original shape, but the modern notion of resilience of systems seems to have emerged in the discipline of ecology in the mid-1970s, with the publication of a now-widely cited paper on the topic by Canadian ecologist C.S. Holling (1973). Holling made a point of distinguishing between two ways of understanding system resilience— an engineering perspective that assumes a system has a single, well-defined equilibrium state that it can return to after a disruption, and an ecological perspective that sees systems as having multiple, dynamic equilibrium states. In engineered systems, Holling and his colleagues have argued, resilience can be defined as the time required to return to normal function after a disruption, while in ecological systems, resilience is the ability of a system to avoid being pushed over the edge into an alternative equilibrium regime (Folke 2006; Gunderson 2000; Holling 1996). In a disciplinary reversal, these definitions are now widely cited in the engineering literature as a way of distinguishing whether a particular resilience project is treating an engineered system in the classical manner or treating it as a complex, quasi-ecological system (e.g. Blackmore and Plant 2008; Madni and Jackson 2009). Within ecology, resilience became a central theme for a great deal of work in the area of social-ecological interactions. From ecology and engineering, the concept eventually migrated into the field of disaster research, a domain of interdisciplinary research dominated by engineers and social scientists. In this field, it became the basis of a new focus on the resilience of human communities, including the infrastructure systems that enable them to function (Bruneau et al. 2003; Norris et al. 2008; Cutter et al. 2008). Disaster researchers, in turn, seem to have introduced the term into the DHS lexicon, although the exact sequence of events at that point is pretty speculative.

There is little consensus, even within specific research traditions, on what properties of a system make it resilient. Madni and Jackson (2009) list a number of resilience heuristics that have been proposed in the engineering literature, in-

PHOTO COURTESY OF U.S. ARMY

cluding functional redundancy, physical redundancy, ability to reorganize, human-in-the-loop when needed, predictability of system behavior, complexity avoidance, graceful degradation, inspectability, and ability to learn or adapt. As this list indicates, resilience is generally closely linked to ideas about system complexity, self-organization, and adaptability.

So, origins aside, why has resilience become the latest word in homeland security? What is its appeal, and why does it make sense to people at this point in history? I think there are four key reasons for its ascension.

The first is that resilience is a good fit with prevailing assumptions about the nature of infrastructure and its sensitivity to harm. In the 20th century, the term infrastructure emerged as a military concept, and was first problematized in terms of protecting distinct infrastructure assets from harm. During the Cold War, a systems view of infrastructure emerged, with a focus on civil defense and ensuring that infrastructure systems, as whole entities, could survive an attack. This view became the basis of the all-hazards "critical infrastructure protection" paradigm that emerged in the 1990s and remains the basis of much homeland security activity (Collier and Lakoff 2008). More recently, however, there has been a movement toward conceptualizing infrastructure systems not just as systems, but as complex networks with dynamic behavior and many interdependencies that could be exploited by adversaries. For example, DHS's National Infrastructure Simulation and Analysis Center (NISAC), at Los Alamos and Sandia National Laboratories, is largely dedicated to simulating the dynamics of infrastructure network disruption, including the impact of interdependencies between systems. Resilience, with its connotation of adaptation and bouncing back in the face of disruption, captures this sense of the dynamics of a complex network.

A recent example of how resilience has become associated with this network perspective is a DHS call for proposals to enhance community resilience, which focuses on social network analysis as the main tool for predicting community response to disasters (Department of Homeland

Security 2010). This suggests the possibility that both social and technological elements of resilience may eventually be encompassed within the network metaphor of complex system behavior.

The second reason resilience works so well for the homeland security community is that it appears more "pro-active"—to use contemporary management-speak—than the alternatives, vulnerability and protection (Wilbanks 2010). Vulnerability might be seen as implying weakness, while protection implies a purely defensive stance. Resilience, on the other hand, enables patriotic appeals to American values. To quote Jeanette Napolitano again,

America is a strong nation. And we are a resilient nation. But … we can't guarantee there won't be another successful terrorist attack … if that attack comes, our enemies will still not have succeeded, because our nation is too strong, and too resilient, to ever cower before a small group of violent extremists. We have always rebounded from hardships and challenges, and come together as a people to overcome disasters, attacks, and war. And we will do so again (Napolitano, 2010).

So, while the concept of resilience may have originally come out of a very academic context, it is apparent here that part of its success as a term lies in its ability to be mobilized in a explicitly political rhetoric of national identity.

Third, I wonder if the term resilience is becoming popular not just because of its optimistic, can-do connotations, but also because it taps into a darker vein of contemporary anxiety in wealthy Western countries like the United States. By most indicators, the U.S. is not a particularly vulnerable country (though of course vulnerability is not evenly distributed within the population). While it is subject to hurricanes, earthquakes, and other natural hazards, and is now understood to be at some risk from terrorist attacks, the U.S. generally has the infrastructure and resources in place to prevent large numbers of casualties and mitigate the social and economic impacts of most foreseeable natural disasters or hostile acts. Our large, technologically advanced military also ensures that we have the defensive resources to counter all but the most determined adversaries.

But first the 9/11 attacks, and then Hurricane Katrina, have raised questions about the stability of these systems. Could it be (we may fear) that even with the vast resources at our disposal, and with the best of intentions, there is still some crucial piece missing, some aspect of our way of life that puts us at greater risk than we should be? Perhaps a brittleness, a disconnectedness, a lack of cohesiveness as a society that creates weak points that could bring the whole system down? If I'm not mistaken, these kind of doubts hover on the periphery of much of our national

---

Vulnerability might be seen as implying weakness. Protection implies a purely defensive stance. Resilience, on the other hand, enables patriotic appeals to American values.

---

discourse on homeland security. Resilience—particularly the concept of community resilience—is all about developing the means to knit communities more tightly together, strengthening both material and social ties and creating a stronger sense of solidarity. Resilience, in this sense, represents the inverse, the negation, of some of the most characteristic fears of modern Western societies, giving it additional rhetorical power.

Finally, related concepts, like vulnerability, have a tendency to bring up social inequalities. Studies of vulnerability show that it is minorities, the poor, the elderly and the disabled who are at greatest risk of harm from disasters. This often is taken to imply redistributive solutions, which in the United States makes it unlikely to form the basis of a political consensus. Resilience, on the other hand, implies a system where community members come together as equals to solve important problems and resolve deep anxieties in a cooperative, "pro-active" spirit, which is much more likely to be perceived as politically neutral.

In summary, resilience has become popular because it works as a "boundary object" (Star and Griesemer 1989): that is, an entity that has meaning and rhetorical utility for a wide range of communities, including academic ecology, engineering, and social sciences; the developers of infrastructure and social network simulations for homeland security applications; and DHS administrators and politicians promoting national security agendas. It provides a common rubric under which these communities can talk to each other and the public, avoiding potential controversies while responding to the characteristic anxieties of our time. □

BENJAMIN SIMS *is technical staff member at the Los Alamos National Laboratory.*

logis-tics' liabil-ities

BY DEBORAH COWEN

IN THE MIDST OF CRISIS, public debate about the future of the economy has largely focused on the systemic vulnerability of finance systems. Yet, a different kind of concern with systemic economic risk has preoccupied a set of global professionals and technical experts for the last decade. This other economic vulnerability stems from the material flows of 'stuff' that constitute trade: the cargo movement of the global logistics system. The deepening interdependency of firms and sectors within supply chains has increasingly been framed as a problem of systemic risk. As Rice and Caniato (2003:4) assert, "If one firm fails in the supply network, the entire network performance is at risk." Efforts to protect commodity flows have given rise to a whole new form and field of security. Military and civilian authorities from public and private sectors are actively assembling a global architecture of 'supply chain security' that aims to keep *stuff* circulating.

Supply chain security takes shape through national and supranational programs that aim to govern events and forces that may disrupt trade flows—labour actions, volcanic eruptions, acts of 'piracy', and even the national border (see Cowen 2010). Because it is oriented towards threats that may be impossible to predict, supply chain security mobilizes pre-emption techniques to mitigate vulnerability (see Cooper 2006, Amoore and De Goede 2008), and preparedness measures to build resilience and recover circulation in the wake of disruption (see Collier and Lakoff 2007, Pettit et. al. 2010). Supply chain security initiatives rely on risk management to identify dangerous goods and disruptive people and keep them away from circulatory systems, alternately targeting high-risk containers, shippers, and workers. But military deployment is also part of the paradigm: naval forces police trade routes in the Gulf of Aden. The mix of military and civilian security is a feature of the transnational geography of supply chains. Indeed, what unites supply chain security initiatives is the space of the circulatory system that extends "from the factory gate in a foreign country to the final destination of the product" (Haveman and Shatz, 2006: 1).

Despite this recent flurry of activity, concern for the systemic vulnerability of logistics systems can be traced back to the 'revolution in logistics' of fifty years ago. Logistics was once one of three modern military arts alongside tactics and strategy. It was the important but unglamorous work of getting 'men and materials' to the front (Jomini 1862). By WWI, transporting troops, technologies, and the fuel for both to the battlefields gained greater importance; logistics ascended from a residual to commanding role in military strategy (DeLanda 1991: 105). After the Second World War logistics was drawing increased attention from forces beyond the bounds of the military. Business managers were convinced that this military art would become a profitable business science. Management guru Peter Drucker (1962: 72) identified logistics and physical distribution as the economy's "Last Dark Continent." He said, "we know little more about distribution today than Napoleon's contemporaries knew about the interior of Africa." Military and colonial metaphors pervade the field even in its civilian form, and it was collaborations between military and business leaders that helped usher in the 'revolution' in the field. Robert McNamara created the Logistics Management Institute (LMI) in 1962 to exploit "the same type of fresh thinking on logistics that is being provided by groups such as Rand on technical and operational matters" (LMI n.d.). The founding of the LMI with a powerful board that included military and civilian directors like Drucker, was both an element in this retooling of logistics and a symbol of its growing influence.

The single most important shift in logistics thought and practice in the early postwar period was the introduction of "systems thinking" or a "systems perspective" (Smykay & Lalonde 1967, LaLonde, Gabner & Robeson 1970). In fact, until the early 1960s the field was known as 'physical distribution management,' defined by the American Marketing Association in 1948 as, "the movement and handling of goods from the point of production to the point of consumption." Systems thinking gave rise to a new approach known as 'integrated distribution management,' a new name for the field 'business logistics,' and importantly, a re-scaled space of action. As Smykay and LaLonde (1967) explain, "under the systems concept, attention is focused upon the total action of a function rather than upon its individual components." Distribution was redefined as an element of the production process rather than a discrete function that followed. As figure 1 below suggests, 'business logistics' brought the entire system of production and distribution into focus. By the end of the revolutionary 1960s, business logistics was defined as "a total approach to the management of all activities involved in physically acquiring, moving and storing raw materials, in-process inventory, and finished goods inventory from the point of origin to the point of use or consumption" (Lalonde, Grabner and Robeson 1970: 43).

WHILE SYSTEMS THOUGHT is recognized as pivotal to the transformation of the field, the sources of this thought are conspicuously absent in industry histories. As Bowersox (1969: 64) explains, "It is difficult to trace the exact origins of the systems approach to problem solving." In fact, it was both systems thought and 'total cost analysis' that were highlighted in discussions of 'integrated distribution management,' yet connection between them remains unexplored. In practice, total cost may have been the applied means through which systems thinking entered the field. The connections become clear in the operation and effects of 'total cost.' In an influential article LeKashman and Stolle explained, "the real cost of distribution includes much more than what most companies consider when they attempt to deal with distribution costs" (1965: 34). They explained that costs which "never appear as distribution costs on any financial or operating report, but show up unidentified and unexplained at different times and in assorted places—in purchasing, in production, in paperwork processing-anywhere and everywhere in the business," are in fact, "intimately interrelated, linked together by one common bond. They all result from the way the company distributes its products" (ibid: 33). Functions previously distinguished from distribution were now counted as part of its total cost, as figure 2 suggests. Calculations that would be impossibly labor intensive were suddenly more manageable with computers. Using total cost, figure 2 shows how a firm can find opportunities to increase profits that it "could not have identified or taken advantage of in any other way" (ibid: 38), and the new solutions to logistics problems that were inherently geographic (e.g. number of warehouses, location of production, mode of transport, etc). This 'interdisciplinary' analysis required the support of top management (ibid. 45), thus propelling logistics to a much higher level of authority within the firm.

If total cost was in fact a practical application of systems thinking, then the source of systems in early logistics thought becomes clear. Total cost analysis was developed by researchers at the RAND Corporation as part of their early operations research. The concept and methods stem directly from RAND's work on Air Force weapons systems in the 1950s (see Fisher 1956). This suggests not the militarization of business, but rather a persistent entanglement of market and military. For decades military strategy was fueled by logistics, and now with the adoption of total cost, logistics started to drive *business* strategy.

The rise of integrated distribution management spurred by total cost constituted the revolution in logistics and put the spatial organization of the firm directly into question. Previously, "the typical analysis would be: x tons of widgets must be shipped from A to B; what is the cheapest full-distribution cost mode to ship by?" the new ap-

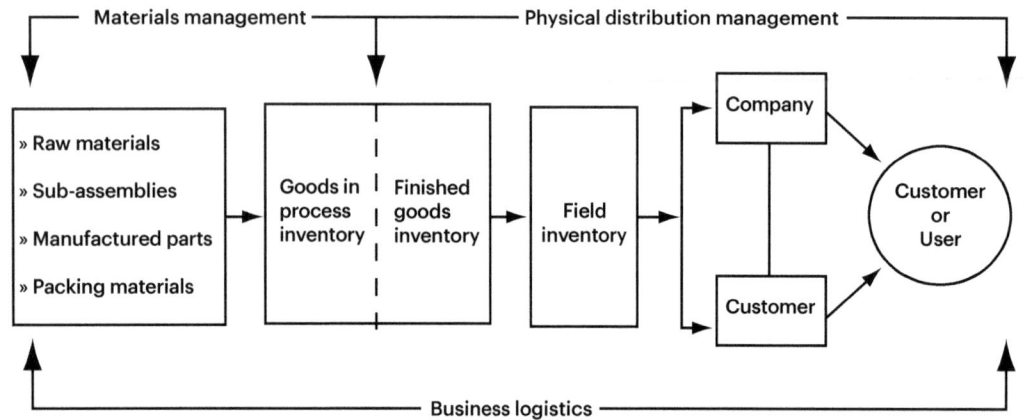

FIG. 1 Alternative orientation to integrated distribution management.
Source: Lalonde, B., Grabner, J., and Robeson, J. (1970) "Integrated Distribution Management: A Management Perspective," International Journal of Physical Distribution. 1: 43.

proach, "would ask questions of whether x was the best amount to ship and whether to ship from point A to point B was the proper origin and destination pair" (Allen 1997: 114). From a least-cost analysis of discrete segments of commodity distribution, logistics became a science of value-added through circulatory systems. By reframing the way that economic space was conceived and calculated, business logistics was critical in remaking of geographies of capitalist production and distribution at a global scale.

Globalized logistics further relied on the shipping container and intermodal infrastructure. These technologies also had a military genesis; the foundations for both containerization and the development of Just-in-Time production techniques stem from the Unites States military's work in Japan and Korea after WWII (Reifer 2004). Underpinned by the deregulation of the transport sector and supranational trade agreements, the last three decades have seen dramatic growth in cross border cargo flows. However, a system built on the speedy circulation of cargo through smooth space also entails new forms of vulnerability. Disruption is the Achilles heel of global logistics systems.

WHILE MANY TYPES of events are now understood to constitute systemic risk, the particular events that prompted the formulation of 'supply chain security' were those of September 2001. Yet it was not the events of September 11– the loss of life, the destruction of urban infrastructure, or even the trespass of state sovereignty that were definitive in its genesis. In the world of logistics and supply chain management, trade disruption (not the twin towers) was the key casualty of 2001. It was the events of September 12, 13, and after – the closure of the American border, the collapse of cargo flow, and the deep impact on trade, particularly in the cross-border auto industry (see CRS 2005: 6, Flynn 2003: 115)—that marked the crisis and prompted response. The immediate cost of delay was calculated at the scale of the individual truck, by port and by gateway, by sector, and for the economy as a whole (see Globerman and Storer 2009, CRS 2002). But in addition to the immediate costs of disruption from border closure there was mounting concern for the longer term costs associated with post-September 11 border tightening. For a system based not simply on connectivity, but speed of connectivity, border security can itself be a source of *insecurity* for the supply chain. This concern for fast flow is precisely why risk-based approaches have been the cornerstone of supply chain security initiatives.

Efforts to secure logistics systems through pre-emption and preparedness provoke questions about the relationship between economy and future life. The move to include protection of global trade as a pillar of national security stems from the central role that trade plays in reproducing a corporate managed and transnationally networked 'way of life'. Yet, a slippage occurs where protection of the economy as a route to protection of life is replaced with the protection of the economy as protection of life itself. Writing in 1966, Wildavsky offered a compelling critique of the "encroachment of economics on politics" that he saw in cost-benefit analysis, systems analysis and project budgeting. He suggested that the economizer, "claims no special interest in or expertise concerning the decision apparatus outside of the market place," yet "pursues efficiency to the heart of the political system." Wildavsky saw a danger in the replacement of objectives with efficiency and the relativization of means and ends. But the rise of 'techné,' the conflation of ends with means, of strategy with logistics, is precisely the achievement of business logistics. The move to govern supply as a problem of security is a further attempt to remove it from the realm of political contestation – *to make economy policy*. Yet disruption is a profoundly political tactic, for instance of workers protesting graphic deaths on the docks associated with demands for higher productivity in California's ports, or of 'Somali pirates' contesting the European dumping of toxic waste in the Gulf. These disparate groups and many others are both governed as threats to the security of supply, concealing complex social worlds animated by the violence of efficient global trade. There are thus heavy stakes in the technical, even technocratic debates over the protection of logistics from systemic failure. ☐

DEBORAH COWEN *is at the University of Toronto.*

ACKNOWLEDGEMENTS:
My sincere thanks go to Stephen Collier, Chris Kelty, and especially Andy Lakoff for extremely productive questions and comments on earlier drafts.

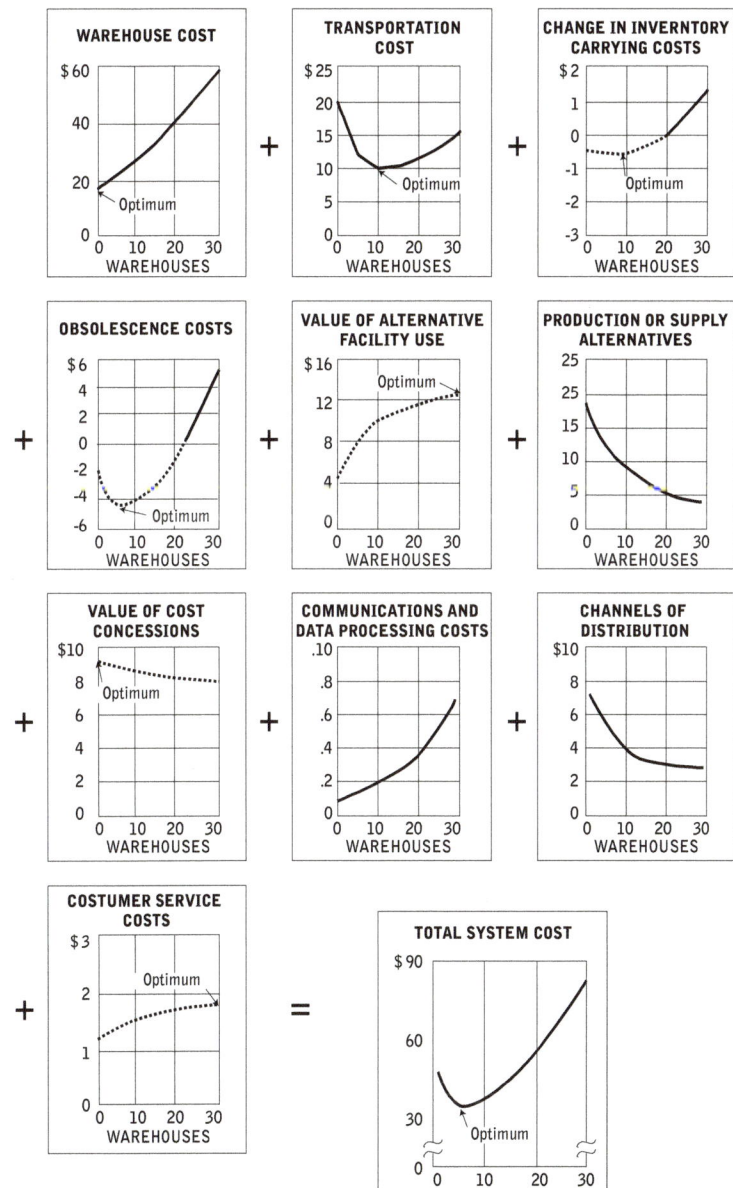

FIGURE 2 The Total Cost Approach. Source: LeKashman, R. and Stolle, J.F. (1965) "The Total Cost Approach to Distribution." *Business Horizons.* Winter: 33-46.

SYSTEMS AT RISK AS RISK TO THE SYSTEM

BY MYRIAM DUNN CAVELTY

SYSTEMIC RISK IN FINANCE refers to at least three things, according to George G. Kaufman and Kenneth E. Scott: It connotes a macro shock that produces nearly simultaneous, large, adverse effects in most or all of the domestic economy or even international financial system. It can also refer to the risk of a chain reaction of falling interconnected dominos or a type of spillover that involves weaker and more indirect connections.

In this short essay, I would like to move beyond this more recent and specific articulation of systemic risk in the financial sector by looking at a broader, though closely related kind: The potential for large-scale disasters or catastrophes characterized by both extreme uncertainty and a potential for extensive and perhaps irreversible harm. This type of systemic risk takes center stage in the highly publicized OECD report on 'Emerging Systemic Risks' (2003). The report with its focus on cross-sectoral risk management issues was occasioned by a number of events such as severe storms, the BSE crisis, major blackouts, and last but not least 9/11. It is influenced by German sociologist Ulrich Beck, who coined the term 'World Risk Society', a society responsible for and faced with universal risks with the potential for the gravest of consequences, which he himself occasionally calls systemic risks to contrast it from individual, local or localized risks.

In specific, the report describes 'a marked future increase in the probability of major vital systems (technological, infrastructural, ecological, etc.) being severely damaged by a single catastrophic event (natural or man-made), or a complex chain of events' (page 32). A systemic risk is defined as one that affects 'the systems on which society depends' (page 30). In the policy domain, these 'systems on which society depends' are usually called critical infrastructures and the need to protect them is a contemporary preoccupation among many policymakers. If we compare the lists of critical sectors identified in various countries, we most often find finance, government services, telecommunication, electricity, health services, transportation, logistics and distribution, and water supply. The systemic risk to the financial sector can therefore be seen as specific and very prominent variant of the larger critical infrastructure debate.

Interestingly enough, the word-conglomerate 'systemic risk' is not native to the critical infrastructure protection (CIP) debate itself, but its two components 'system' and 'risk' are.

System: Infrastructures are always depicted as systems and networks. In a variety of disciplines, particularly the natural and the information sciences, different kinds of systems have been studied at least since the 1940s. Systems research is mainly interested in the behavior of systems be they ordered, chaotic or complex. All three types have relevance for system risk thinking, but it is research on so-called complex adaptive systems (systems that self-organize, change and adapt to the broader environment) that has provided most of the vocabulary for the systemic risk language. CIP practitioners are particularly concerned about two types of system effects: cascades and surprise effects. Cascade effects are those that produce a chain of events that cross geography, time, and various types of systems; surprise effects are unexpected events that arise out of interactions between agents and the negative and positive feedback loops produced through this interaction.

Risk: Because CIP is primarily concerned with technical systems, it is the analytical frameworks developed for accidents with hazardous materials in the chemical industry and nuclear power plants that provide the backdrop for how risks are primarily approached in this debate. According to the standard definition of risk found in the technical domain, it is a function of the *likelihood* of a given *threat source* displaying a particular potential *vulnerability*, and the resulting *impact* of that adverse event. The concept of vulnerability, and more specifically, system-vulnerability, takes center-stage in this. Outcomes of the risk assessment process are used to provide guidance on the areas of highest risk, and to devise policies and plans to ensure that systems are appropriately protected.

The problem with this risk conception is that it only works for systems with clear boundaries that *can* be managed. The reality looks a little different, though: individual infrastructure systems are increasingly bridged and interlinked by information-pathways. Continuing reliance on information technologies for their control and maintenance brings forth an increasing number of networks, nodes, and growing interdependencies in and among these systems. The result is a convergence between two previously separate traditions: of system-vulnerability thinking and complexity theory. The two types of system effects described above are where the notion of system meets the notion of risk: By its very nature, a (complex) system contains the risk of large-scale, catastrophic events that are not bounded or localized, but sweeping. Therefore, the very connectedness of infrastructures poses dangers in terms of the speed and ferocity with which perturbations within them can cascade into major disasters.

Advances in information and communication technology have thus augmented the potential for major disaster (or systemic risk) in critical infrastructures by vastly increasing the possibility for local risks to mutate into systemic risks. In addition, the cyber-moment has elevated the discourse to another urgency-level through a change in the spatial dimension of the threat. In the 1980s, the contemporary CIP discourse began in the US government from a concern with government information systems or rather, the classified information residing on them, which seemed easy prey for tech savvy foreign intelligence agencies, a fear based on various well-publicized break-ins (by teenage boys in most cases). In the late 1980s and especially the 1990s, widespread fear took root in the strategic community that adversaries likely to fail against the US war machine might instead plan to bring the US to its knees by striking against vital points at home, namely, critical infrastructures. Laws of nature, especially physics, do not apply in cyberspace; there are no linear distances, no bodies and no physical co-presences. 'Computer weapons' seemed to reformulate space into something no longer embedded into place or presence. This results in two significant characteristics of the threat representation: First, the protective capacity of space is obliterated; there is no place that is safe from an attack or from catastrophic breakdown in general. Second, the threat becomes quasi universal because it is now everywhere.

At the same time, the image of modern critical infrastructures is one in which it becomes futile to try and separate the human from the technological. Technology is not simply a tool that makes life livable: rather, technologies become constitutive of novel forms of a complex subjectivity, which is characterized by an inseparable ensemble of material and human elements. From this 'ecological' understanding of subjectivity, a specific image of society emerges: society becomes inseparable from critical infrastructure networks. This way, systemic risks understood as risks to critical infrastructure systems are risks to the entire system of modern life and being.

This view is ultimately problematic, because it results in generalized and highly diffuse anxiety based on a sense of 'imminent but inexact catastrophe', lurking just beneath the surface of everyday life. The downside of this is that the systemic risk debate as studied in this essay is reduced to a distressing limbo state of not-safe-but-waiting-for-destruction/disaster, a disaster, which is construed as inevitable. But one of the great lessons of risk sociology is that risks 'are' not, they are made by humans and more importantly, as they are not manifest yet but situated in a highly uncertain future, they can be shaped by human choices in the present. What the systemic risk debate needs to be politically stimulating rather than a fear and anxiety trap is a move away from a doomsday-automatism linked to propensities of system effects towards a focus on human action and human responsibility. □

MYRIAM DUNN CAVELTY *is Senior Researcher at Eldgenössische Technische Hochschule in Zurich.*

HOW SHIT HAPPENS

AUDIT SYSTEMS AND SEWER STATES LEAD TO TAINTED BEEF

BY ELIZABETH CULLEN DUNN

WE LIVE IN A RISK SOCIETY. On a never-ending search-and-destroy mission to eliminate sources of potential harm, we constantly develop new systems to identify it and mitigate it. But do risk management systems make us safer? Or do they instead increase the very risks they are meant to eliminate?

Questions about how Americans find, mitigate and create risks are apparent on a daily basis in the industrialized food system. Since 1993, when *E. coli O157:H7* was found in Jack in the Box hamburgers, there has been a multi-state outbreak of food-borne illness nearly every year. From a 25 million pound recall of beef in 2002, to an outbreak linked to bagged spinach in 2006, from the 2009 discovery of Salmonella–laced peanut butter in 2009 to an outbreak of Listeria linked to chopped celery in 2010, it seems that the risk of contaminated food and the fear that goes with it have become inevitable in America's industrialized food system.

The food industry has treated bacteriological contamination as a technical problem, and has responded with new technologies to ensure food safety, including carcass washes, acid dips, and even radiation. Yet, the bacteria seem to constantly overflow the technological solutions meant to contain them. Why can't the industry seem to control the spread of disease? Why can't the federal government seem to make food safe? Is the public's beef really only with beef, or do contemporary worries over microbiological pathogens like *E. coli* show deep public discomfort with more than just food?

THE PROBLEM IS that because food-borne illness arises from a spatial ecology created by a highly consolidated food system, the microbes of disease exceed mere technological fixes. In the beef industry, for example, 85% of the US market is controlled by four companies that have established massive feedlots where thousands of cattle stand nose-to-tail in their own feces. These cattle are killed in high-speed slaughterhouses, where a single slip of a worker's knife into the intestines of an animal carrying O157:H7 could contaminate the entire river of meat made by combining flesh from thousands of animals into a continuous flowing stream of ground beef.

The USDA has responded to the problem of the material system of food production with an administrative system designed to mitigate risk. The Hazards Analysis of Critical Control Points (HACCP) system requires meatpackers to analyze their production processes for potential risks, places where pathogens might be introduced, or steps where pathogens might be killed (e.g. a cooking step where the meat is raised to temperatures that destroy the bacteria). Then the packers are supposed to label these steps as "critical control points," or CCPs, and establish "critical limits" for each of them. Under HACCP, USDA inspectors don't test the meat at all—in fact, under the terms of the 5th Circuit Court decision in *Supreme Beef vs. USDA*, the USDA has no power to test beef for microbial contamination. Instead, USDA inspectors inspect the logs detailing the measurements of the CCPs. Audits are supposed to create trust in the food system by creating "transparency." That is, they purport to have a one-to-one correspondence with what actually goes on in a firm, granting auditors (the USDA) and consumers the ability to look onto the kill floor and the production line and see what actually happens there. Modern power is thus based on more than the gaze, on more than the watchful eye, and on more than mere surveillance and punishment: it is based on the ability to purify, to remove excess, corruption and putrefaction from view and sweep it away.

These audits seek to define specific, spatially delimited points in the production process where new technologies can be brought in to fix contamination. But because the problem comes from the economic structure of meatpacking and the large-scale spaces of food production it engenders, microbial contamination seems to constantly spill into new spaces even as HACCP seeks to eliminate it. Outbreak after outbreak forces firms and regulators to keep searching the production process to find "reservoirs of disease," or places where microbes are lurking. Because they are forced by the HACCP system to find more and more "critical control points" where bacteria might be, packers have been finding more places where microbes can be identified and destroyed. Where once *E. coli O157:H7* was only in the cows' intestines, now it appears to overflow that fragile membrane and to spill into noses pressed up to other cows' rumps, onto hides, into water troughs that flow among corrals, and into the trucks that bring animals from different herds together to transport them to the packing plant. It is found not just in the packing plant, but in the lairage outside it, at the feedyard, and on ranches—all spaces that USDA has no jurisdiction over.

Clearly, *E. coli*'s ability to proliferate in space exceeds the state's ability to control it. Just as *E. coli* is being seen now as overflowing the intestine, the container which bounds excrement, so too is *E. coli* and the excrement that bears

Modern power is ... based on the ability to purify, to remove excess, corruption and putrefaction from view and sweep it away.

it overflowing the audit system, the system the state claims is a sewer which could transmute excrement into numbers, contain disease, and carry away pathogenic waste. So, paradoxically, although the HACCP system is meant to create trust, what it really creates is anxiety. It reveals overflows of filth and zones of wildness, like the ranch, the trough, and the cow's rump, where contamination is rampant. Like all audit systems premised on the detection of risk, HACCp impels the state not only to respond to external crises, but to continually seek out such crises in order to prove its own ability to provide security and to convince the population of the need for regulation. Risk in the food system is thus not just a continually expanding problem, but one created by the very system meant to contain it. □

ELIZABETH CULLEN DUNN *is Associate Professor of Geography at University of Colorado at Boulder.*

The Morris worm was released in November of 1988. It was launched surreptitiously from an MIT computer by graduate student Robert Tappan Morris at Cornell University, and spread to internet-connected computers running the BSD variant of UNIX. The worm was designed to be undetectable, but a design flaw led it to create far more copies of itself than Morris estimated, and resulted in the drastic over-taxing of all the computers on which it was installed. This in turn allowed for its immediate detection and the repair of the flaws that it exploited.

THE MORRIS WORM

BY CHRISTOPHER M. KELTY

THE MORRIS WORM was not a destructive worm, it only caused computers to slow and buckle under the weight of unnecessary processing. Nor was the intent of Morris clear: some speculate that the release was either premature or accidental (Spafford 1989; Eisenberg et. al. 1989). Nonetheless the event precipitated two different responses that have since become the focus of much attention and concern over the intervening years. Exploring these two responses reveals something about what "systemic risk" might or might not mean in the context of the Internet and how it relates to other uses of the concept.

The first and most direct response was that Morris became the first individual to be tried under the new Computer Fraud and Abuse Act of 1986, 18 U.S. Code Section 1030(a)(5)(A). Morris was tried, convicted and sentenced to three years of probation, 400 hours of community service, a fine of $10,050, and the costs of his supervision. The case was appealed, and the conviction upheld.

The second response was the creation by Defense Advanced Research Projects Agency (DARPA) of the Computer Emergency Response Team (CERT), in order to coordinate information and responses to computer vulnerabilities and security.

OF THE FIRST RESPONSE—the criminal prosecution—a couple of things stand out. The first is the continuing moral ambivalence about Morris' intentions. On the one hand, what Morris did, objectively, was to force certain security vulnerabilities to be fixed by writing a program that publicly exploited them. As the author of one official investigation, Eugene Spafford, pointed out, the code contained no commands that would harm a computer on which it ran, only commands intended to exploit vulnerabilities that allowed the code to copy itself and spread. On the other hand, his conviction for Fraud and Abuse clearly sends a different message—that this was a criminal act, and as the law had it, one that threatened not just citizens, but the federal government itself.

The practice of publicly demonstrating exploitable vulnerabilities in order to force vendors and system administrators to fix their systems has become established in the academic field of computer science, though it has been largely restricted to the publication of papers that demonstrate how to do it, rather than the release of software that actually does so. This puts Morris, who is now employed at MIT's AI lab and a successful researcher, squarely in the camp of what is known colloquially as "white hat hackers"—hackers, including both academic and corporate employees, who (demonstrate how to) exploit vulnerabilities in order to *make publicly visible* security flaws that need fixing. Morris' worm, from this standpoint looks more like incompetence as a white hat hacker, than the criminal action of a black hat hacker.[2] The moral ambivalence mirrors that around many of the hacker-cum-Silicon Valley success stories that might be cited in this instance.

In terms of the criminality of the Morris worm, one might ask: is the risk that such actions pose a *systemic* risk? The Morris Worm was neither designed to, nor did it cause harm of a particular sort (theft of documents or information, deletion or destructive interference, spam, porn, terrorist intervention, etc.). Rather, its effect was more general in that it caused the Internet, as a collection of interconnected computers, to do something it was not designed to do, and as a result, slow down or cease to function properly.

But is such an effect an issue of "systemic risk?" In part the answer may rest on what is defined as the system, and in particular whether the *system* or the *risk* is perceived as the "emergent" property (i.e. something which emerges through the interaction of parts, but cannot be reduced to, or predicted by those interactions). In the case of the Internet, the system itself is the emergent part: what we call the Internet is only the effect of tens of millions of devices all operating with standardized software-based protocols that govern how they connect, transfer information and disconnect. The platform that emerges is flexible, reconfigurable, asynchronous and without any pre-designed structure to it. Worms and viruses affect this emergent system by affecting software on many particular computers; in the case of the Morris worm, by changing the function of the email management software called `sendmail`, and the name lookup service called `finger`. The particular vulnerabilities that allow a worm or virus to do this (such as "buffer overflow" vulnerabilities) are the proper quarry of the computer security researcher.

The terminology of *worms* and *viruses* express different conceptions of propagation in terms of computer programs. Viruses operate on the analogy of biological viruses by inserting a bit of code into a running program which exploits a vulnerability to allow it to replicate, and potentially, to do harm. A worm by contrast (shortened from tapeworm) is a complete program more like a parasite or symbiont; it reproduces itself via the very vulnerabilities that it exploits. In both cases, individual (networked) computers are the locus and necessary starting point: because networked operating system software is designed to create myriad forms of connections with other computers, and hence bring a network into being, it can be exploited to spread worms and viruses similar to how infections or rumors spread. There is no difference, therefore, between the risk to all of the infected computers combined, and the risk to the "system" understood as the network that emerges out of the interconnection of machines. Or to put it differently, security researchers understand the nature of the risk of a virus or worm to be simply the risk posed by a virus to a particular computer multiplied by the number of computers that are affected. In this sense, worms or viruses do not pose a *systemic* risk—i.e. a new risk that emerges out of or on top of aggregate risks to known components. Rather they are of a piece with the emergence of the network itself.

Contrast this with systemic risk in a case like catastrophe insurance. In the case of catastrophe insurance it is not necessarily the system that is emergent, but the risk. Individual policies have well-defined risks, but the risk of a portfolio of policies cannot be predicted by the aggregate risk of all the individual policies. Similarly, there is nothing analogous to the Internet as an "emergent network" that results from the issuing of policies—though catastrophe insurance policies can clearly be said to interact at some level (especially when events occur). As such there is a "systemic risk" at play that is different in kind, not only degree, from the risk that pertains to individual policies. The comparison is uneven, however, since the case of insurance already builds on the concept of population-level risk, and not just that of individuals—there is no obvious point of comparison here to the relationship between individual computers and a network.

Nonetheless, the idea that computer security risks are not "emergent" explains the often indignant response of computer security researchers (and white hat hackers) to vulnerabilities: there is no mystery, there is no "emergent risk," the vulnerabilities can and should be fixed by users and vendors by fixing all the individual software components.

There are other uses of "systemic" in the context of computer security. The language of viruses and worms clearly designates a threat to a system understood as an organism. The language of *payloads* (often also used in the biological field) designates the specific threat or violence a virus or worm might visit on a computer and its associated network. At least one paper uses the language of an *ecology* of "security and policy flaws" in which it is possible for worms

---

1 Morris' reputation has suffered little. For many hackers (Kevin Mitnick being the most famous), a conviction is hardly a setback, and in many cases provides a boost to their reputations. Morris is today also a partner in the alternative venture capital firm Y Combinator, where his bio delightfully reads "In 1988 his discovery of buffer overflow first brought the Internet to the attention of the general public."

and viruses to thrive (Weaver et. al. 2003:16): application design, buffer overflows, privileges, application deployed widely, economic costs of development and testing of software, patch deployment, and "monocultures" (i.e. the absence of a diversity of machines and software).

For the most part, the Morris worm—as a problem of hackers, criminals, computer security researchers and software vendors—is concerned with the possibility of understanding, making visible and controlling vulnerabilities in the parts, in order to safeguard an emergent system that forms through their interaction. Risk is almost always equated to vulnerabilities (known and unknown) in this sense.

BY CONTRAST, the other response, the formation of the Computer Emergency Response Team, ties the event of the Morris worm directly to the rise of thinking about critical infrastructure protection. The DARPA funded project, which is headquartered at Carnegie Mellon's Software Engineering Institute, publishes a variety of announcements, analyses, fixes and warnings concerning software and networking vulnerabilities. In 1997 they wrote a report (Ellis et. al. 1997) to the Presidents Commission on Critical Infrastructure Protection that reported a list of problems that CERT has continually encountered (similar to the ecology cited earlier, but not so-named). A handful of publications and presentations that identify problems of interdependency have been published, and the organization has focused some of its energy on creating tools, mechanisms, textbooks and guidelines for "software assurance", as well as topics like "resiliency engineering management" and "vulnerability disclosure."

The rise of "Critical Infrastructure Interdependency" research that began with the publication of Rinaldi et.al. (2001) has grown out of and alongside these institutions. The notion of "infrastructure interdependency" is a more apt conceptual analog to "systemic risk" than are worms and viruses (which in this context look more like specific techniques, rather than events in themselves). CII research suggests that it is not the system that is emergent, but the risk.

Individual systems (or infrastructures) may be emergent, as the Internet is, and even highly designed systems such as the electrical power grid might also exhibit emergent features (Watts and Strogatz 1998). However, it is the interaction between systems or infrastructures that introduces risks that cannot be predicted or reduced to the component parts. CII researchers are therefore

---

The Morris worm reveals something about what "systemic risk" might or might not mean in the context of the Internet.

---

intensely concerned with the concrete points of connection between systems, a much discussed example of which is supervisory control and data acquisition (SCADA) software, especially when it is deployed in the context of the Internet as a tool for managing industrial processes. The "emergent" risk comes from the unpredictable vulnerabilities that obtain when, for instance, electrical power grids are monitored by and dependent upon networked computers. The language of "cascades" and contagious risk appears in this research with as much regularity as it does in the domain of finance (e.g. the bank contagion literature).

For its part, the academic field of computer security research seems to remain at a distance from the related concerns of systemic risk in finance, public health, or defense, despite being well-funded by the likes of DARPA and well-represented by agencies like the National Security Agency (whose National Computer Security Center was for a long period headed by none other than Robert Morris Sr.). For most computer security researchers, flaws and vulnerabilities are confined to the operating system level of networked computers, or at most, extend to social or policy vulnerabilities, such as physical access to computers, poor management of accounts and privileges, or non-existent monitoring of personal computers connected to the Internet. They have historically not been much concerned with the interdependency of two networked systems, like the electrical grid and the Internet. A certain hubris, perhaps, follows from the separation of worms/viruses and their "payload"—and the field is alive with imaginaries about exploitation by evil-doers, rather than collapse or break-down due to normal design or usage. The idea of a "normal accident" is almost completely foreign to existing computer

security research. Intent, even in the attenuated form that resulted in Morris' conviction, is an obsession of this field. By contrast, breakdowns and the failure of software to function as expected has largely been the subject of software engineering, which has been berating itself for a very long time now (40 years, beginning with the famous 1968 NATO report on Software Engineering). Instead of security, such concerns are largely the domain of software development practices, quality assurance systems, and an ever-increasing number of standards intended to manage the problem of poorly designed, poorly performing software.

By way of conclusion, an interesting point of convergence has emerged just in the past year. The recent W32.Stuxnet worm targeted SCADA software made by Siemens used to conduct process engineering and control the operation of large-scale plants, like Iran's new nuclear power plant. It's not at all clear at this point that this should be called an *Internet* worm or virus, because it could not have infected the computers it infected without someone physically inserting a USB stick with the Stuxnet code into a computer running the Siemens SCADA software. The worm replicated itself through an internally networked system and it apparently opens up control to outsiders, but it does not go on to affect the function of the Internet in any way, only the operation of the plant in question. Here, again, the risk is "emergent" but only in the sense that the longstanding attempt to create computer controlled industrial processes has itself produced unpredictable vulnerabilities. At a technical level such vulnerabilities are not different in kind than those the Morris worm exploited: they result from poor engineering, overlooked weaknesses, or poor security practice. But at a more "systemic" level they are different in kind since they affect not only the operation of the computers themselves, but the physical operation of a plant or "interdependent" system. □

CHRISTOPHER KELTY *is Associate Professor at the Center for Society and Genetics and the Department of Information Studies, UCLA.*

THE *BECOMING-INSURABLE* OF TERRORISM RISK IN THE US
IMAGINING SYSTEMIC RISK

BY PHILIP BOUGEN

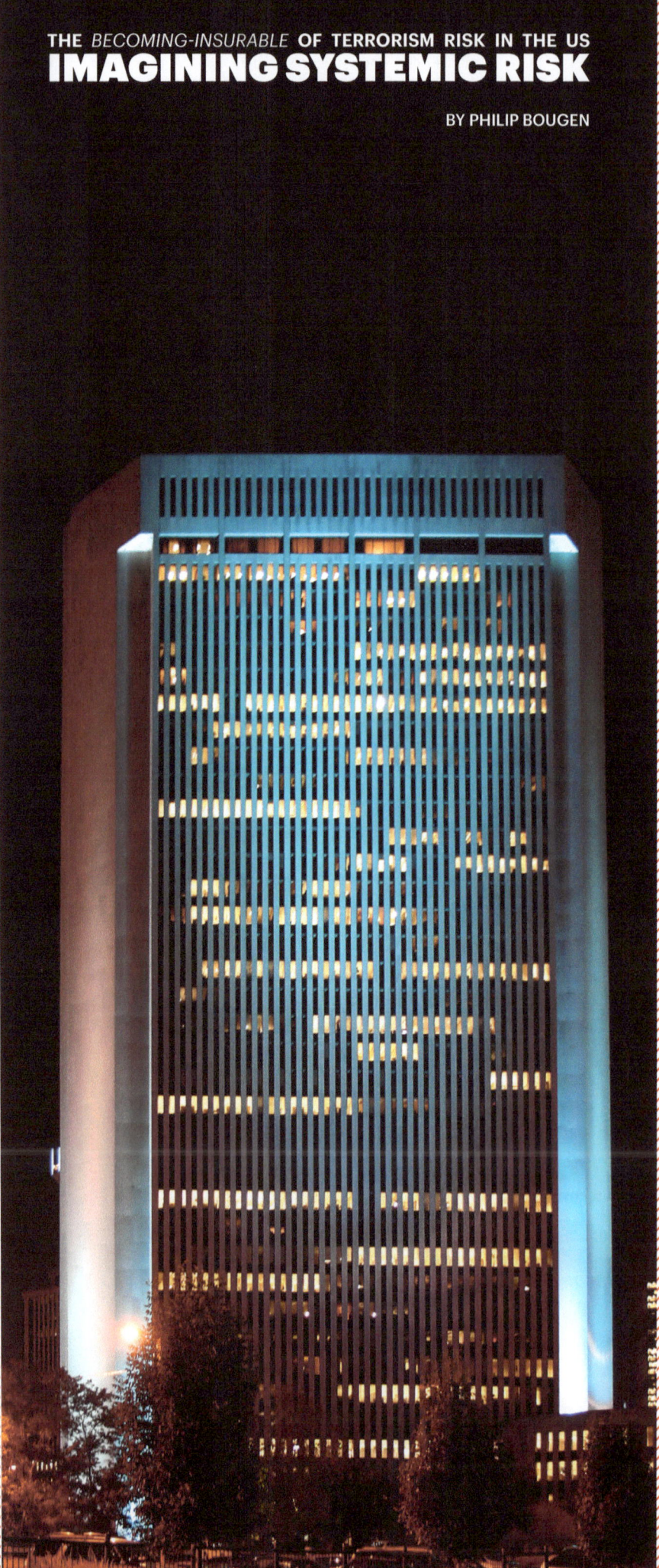

◄**ONE NATIONWIDE PLAZA**
Headquarters of **Nationwide Mutual Insurance Company & Affiliated Companies**, in Columbus, Ohio.

"Where does the boundary lie between the history of knowledge and the history of imagination?"

Michel Foucault

BACKGROUND: The Terrorism Risk Insurance Act (TRIA) enacted into law in 2002 established a formula whereby the private insurance industry and the federal government would share insurable losses in the event of a terrorist attack in the US. Originally enacted for a three-year duration, with explicit recognition of its anticipated temporary status, the Act was extended in 2005 for a further 2 years and again in 2007 for a further seven-year period. The original stated rationales for the Act were:

01 By limiting the potential losses of insurers, the provision of private terrorism risk insurance would be encouraged.

02 A period of federal financial support would provide the insurance industry with an intervening period of time to acquire more knowledge about the insurability of terrorism attacks and develop the statistical tools and actuarial methods to facilitate the private insurance process.
(Insurance Information Institute, 2011)

AFTER 9/11, insurance companies, insured and legislators imagined the risks posed to the future functioning of the national economy by recent events and by the possibility of further terrorist attacks. The specter of a possible systemic risk to the economy was raised. Insurers and reinsurers chastened by their approximate $40 billion compensation payments for 9/11 property damage imagined that "it will be impossible to provide our customers with terrorism coverage" (US House, September 26, 2001, 39). In fact, private sector terrorism risk insurance was being sold by October, 2001. For mor on this see Bougen (2009: 36). Insured either in the form of organizations representing real estate and construction industries (such as American Council for Capital Formation, Associated Contractors of America, American Resort Development Association, Mortgage Bankers Association of America, National Association of Real Estate Investment Trusts, National Association of Realtors, Real Estate Round Table), or owning property considered particularly susceptible to attack, 'trophy targets' (such as Seattle Mariners Baseball Stadium, St. Louis Art Museum, Amtrak, National Geographic Center, Golden Gate Bridge, Hyatt Hotels, Los Vegas Casinos, Disney World, Mall of America, New York Hospitals), imagined the financial consequences of their particular vulnerability to the unavailability of terrorism risk insurance. Legislators imagined the risks to the economy if corporations were unable to insure assets against damages from terrorist attacks: insurance is "the glue which holds our economy together" (Congressional Record, November 29, 2001, H8573).

Had a systemic risk to the US economy emerged? One perhaps consistent with Beck's (1992, 1999, 2002) risk society thesis that without federal financial support, insurers could not and would not want to insure terrorism risk? Nobody knew for certain: imagined realities were at the forefront. Beck attributed uninsurability to the delocalized, incalculable and non-compensable elements of the danger. Delocalized refers to the uncontained effects of misfortune whereby unfavorable consequences 'spill over' into other physical and temporal zones and outside of insurance parameters. Incalculable refers to a resistance to quantitative assessment rendering risk metrics and actuarial calculations as hypothetical. Non-compensable

refers to destruction of such magnitude that monetary restitution no longer proves sufficient. Each of these three suspected impediments to insurability was extensively discussed in legislative hearings. Proponents of TRIA and federal financial support emphasized the plausibility of the impediments while opponents queried their status of intractability as barriers to insurability.

This observation provides a means of thinking about the idea of the becoming-insurable of terrorism risk. The Deleuzian concept of becoming suggests the moving, underdetermined and unfinished process of the insuring of terrorism risk. Becoming also resonates with Foucault's disquiet with strict epistemological demarcations. Becoming is the in-between: for us the boundaries of insurability and non-insurability. An imaginary of the insurability of terrorism: its necessity, feasibility and sustainability. Also an imaginary of non-insurability: its excess, infeasibility and fragility. The becoming insurable of terrorism risk, in particular the role federal funding might play, passed in-between these imaginaries. In doing so, all types of terrorism risk insurance boundaries were explored: the boundaries between risk and uncertainty, between the calculable and non-calculable and between private opportunities and public responsibilities. In slightly different terms, boundaries were explored by imagining the possible systemic risk the unavailability of terrorism risk insurance might pose to the economy and how it might become insurable.

Whilst imagined and often precariously drawn, such boundaries should not be considered as inconsequential: boundaries "transmit and control exchanges between territories" (Richter and Peitgen 1985: 571-572). Present

and future financial relationships between the public as taxpayers, corporations, insurers and reinsurers were shaped by these boundaries: who would provide monies, to whom, when and in what amount in the event of a future attack. What might be considered the financial engineering of systemic risk. An engineering, however, susceptible to continuous re-engineering as different imaginaries of terrorism risk were re-imagined.

Two further observations are relevant. Firstly, the identification of terrorism risk insurance as an issue of economic wellbeing did not fortuitously appear on the legislative agenda: proponents and sponsors with different interests and agendas aligned to promote insurance as a necessary and legitimate legislative concern. Shifting imaginaries of ubiquitous yet ethereal danger marked this terrain. Secondly, possible future terrorism risk insurance arrangements required exploration, formulation and evaluation: an exercise consisting of the imaginative alignments of moving contingent financial relationships. Stated succinctly: imaginaries were employed to construct various scenarios of whether a systemic risk to the functioning of the US economy had emerged.

POSTSCRIPT: *"What is real is the becoming itself... not the supposedly fixed terms through which that which becomes passes"* (Deleuze and Guattari, 1987: 238): *points to the problematic status of assessing whether a risk is systemic and its insurability.* □

PHILIP BOUGEN *is at University of New Mexico.*

SOME BOUNDARIES AND IMAGINARIES IN THE *BECOMING-INSURABLE* OF TERRORISM RISK

A BOUNDARY BETWEEN the indispensable and dispensable status of insurance: Insurance is "critically important not just to insurance companies, agents and brokers, but also to the future viability of literally hundreds of thousands of small and large US businesses" (Statement of the Independent Insurance Agents of America, US House, October 24, 2001: 169).

Proponents of TRIA "speak out of the opposite sides of their mouths... the same people will argue that the creation of a natural catastrophe fund is simply a bailout, that it will supplant the private market, or that taxpayers will be subsidizing high-risk areas" (Representative Brown-Waite from hurricane prone Florida proposing a federal fund similar to TRIA in the event of natural catastrophes, 2007).

A BOUNDARY BETWEEN public responsi-

bility and private opportunity: "Clearly this is just not an insurance issue. This is an issue that will affect our entire economy" (Representative Oxley, Chairman of the House Committee on Financial Services, US House, October 24, 2001: 3).

"The insurance companies see this as an opportunity. A number of records sent back and forth.... have made it clear the time is now to fully exploit the opportunity that was presented by September 11 in terms of creating new companies, creating new entities, and going after capital" (Representative Miller, California, Congressional Record, November29, 2001: 23329).

A BOUNDARY BETWEEN non-calculability and calculability: "Let me begin by stating some very simple facts... We do not know where it is going to occur. We do not know when it is going to occur. We do not know how often it is going to occur. And we do not know how much it is going to cost when it does occur". (Csiszer, President and CEO, Property

Casualty Insurers of America, US House, July 27, 2005: 54).

The insurance industry "can predict, not with precision, because this is not a precise thing... but you can predict... it is doable and is being done (Hunter, Director of Insurance Consumer Federation of America, Senate, May 18, 2004: 69, a vociferous critic of the necessity of TRIA).

A BOUNDARY BETWEEN risk sharing and private choices Whether the market can or cannot do this is not to me the primary concern", the risk "ought to be broadly shared. This is a case for totally socializing the risk" (Representative Frank, Massachusetts, US House, July 27, 2005: pp. 5-6).

The case against risk sharing: "I have farmers in my district, they have chicken houses... Those farmers do not feel like those chicken houses and those chickens need insurance against terrorism" (Representative Bachus, Alabama, Congressional Record, US House, November 29. 2001, H8617).

THE BIKINI ATOLL, 1946
Mushroom-shaped cloud and water column from the under-water *Baker* nuclear explosion of July 25. Chemist Glenn Seaborg, the longest-serving chairman of the Atomic Energy Commission, called Baker "the world's first nuclear disaster."

SYSTEM VULNERABILITY AND THE PROBLEM OF NATIONAL SURVIVAL

PHOTOGRAPH BY UNITED STATES DEPARTMENT OF DEFENSE

BY STEPHEN J. COLLIER AND ANDREW LAKOFF

IN A 1962 LECTURE TO THE WAR INDUSTRIAL COLLEGE, the Director of the US Office of Emergency Planning (OEP), Edward McDermott, described his agency's mission. Charged with preparing the nation for nuclear war, the scope of OEP's responsibility was impressive:

We are really talking about the fundamentals of life on this earth; the elemental problems of safeguarding the food we eat, the fuel we consume, the transportation to maintain a steady flow of commerce, an intricate telecommunications system which will continue to function under all conditions, and perhaps most important, the foundation of constitutional government which underpins our way of life. These are the things that concern the OEP.

While its area of concern was potentially limitless, the OEP approached this vast array of "things" in a distinctive way: as a collection of critical and interdependent systems to be safeguarded against the catastrophic disruption of nuclear attack. In this essay, we briefly describe how, from the mid-1950s to early-1960s, experts and officials charged with preparing for nuclear catastrophe in the United States sought to manage "the fundamentals of life on this earth" by producing a new kind of knowledge that focused on risks to the critical systems that underpinned collective life.

The mission articulated by McDermott was the outcome of a series of discussions and debates that took place over the course of the 1950s among lawmakers, bureaucrats, military planners and technical consultants about how to plan for thermonuclear war. In the wake of the first Soviet H-bomb tests in the early 1950s and in anticipation of the development of intercontinental ballistic missiles, Cold War defense strategists turned their attention to a novel problem: the protection of the nation against a devastating surprise attack. They argued that the traditional emphasis of civil defense on problems of urban preparedness—emergency response, evacuation, and the restoration of local services—was now obsolete. The prospect of a

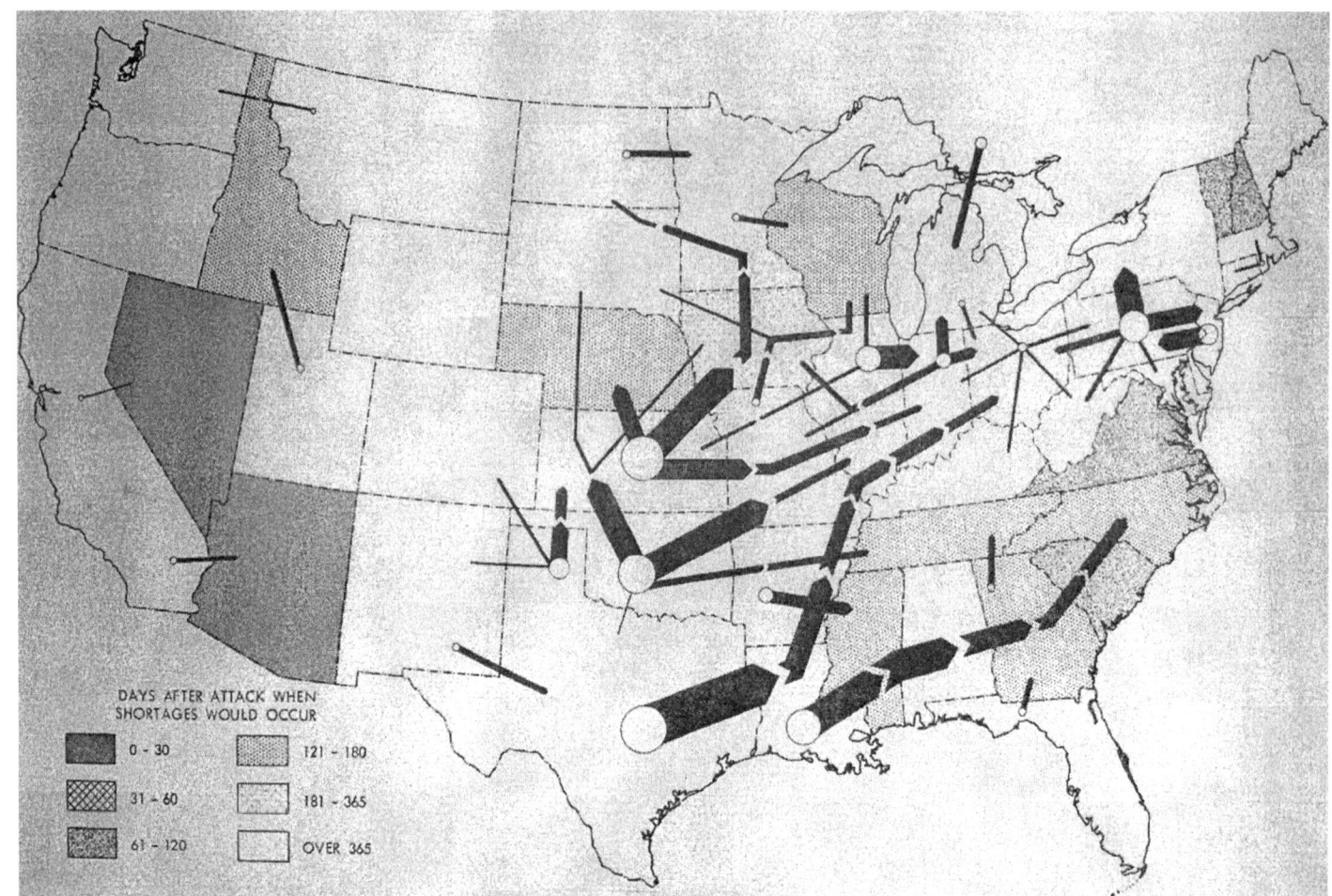

DAYS AFTER ATTACK WHEN
SHORTAGES WOULD OCCUR

▨ 0 – 30	▨ 121 – 180	
▨ 31 – 60	▨ 181 – 365	
▨ 61 – 120	□ OVER 365	

thermonuclear attack heralded destruction on a previously unimaginable scale. Many American cities would be entirely destroyed. Radioactive fallout would make vast areas of the country uninhabitable. The very future of the United States as an economic and political entity would be in doubt. How could one plan for national survival under such circumstances?

A group of thinkers with backgrounds in fields such as strategic bombing theory, mobilization planning, and systems analysis, with access to new computer technology for amassing and processing large amounts of data, offered one response to this challenge. These experts were located both outside of government – in think tanks like the RAND Corporation, the Stanford Research Institute, and the Institute for Defense Analysis—and in key government offices such as the Federal Civil Defense Agency and military research organizations such as the Naval Radiological Defense Laboratory and the Strategic Assessment Committee in the Office of Defense Mobilization. While they did not speak with one voice, there was an emerging consensus in the mid-1950s that it was necessary to focus, in advance of nuclear war, on the vulnerability of the systems that undergirded collective

life: energy networks, industrial facilities, transportation infrastructures, and communications systems, as well as the personnel who operated these systems. Using digital computers, they invented techniques for analyzing collective life as a complex of these vital and vulnerable systems; for modeling how these systems would be affected by nuclear war; and for planning measures that would reduce vulnerability and prepare the government to manage the economy and polity after a nuclear attack.

An early articulation of this "system-vulnerability thinking" can be found in the extensive hearings on non-military defense held by the U.S. House of Representatives Committee on Government Operations in the mid-1950s. During these hearings, experts and officials in fields such as civil defense, mobilization planning, structural engineering, and radiation science testified that existing conceptions of preparedness would have to be radically changed given the prospect of thermonuclear war. The Committee's report on its 1956 Hearings, *Civil Defense for National Survival*, laid out a new framework for domestic preparedness in the age of the thermonuclear threat, oriented toward ensuring the capacity for recovery in the

AFTER THE ATTACK
Post-attack gasoline shortages and interstate products pipeline capacity after minor repairs (From Sanford B. Thayer and Willis W. Shaner, "Effects of Nuclear Attacks on the Petroleum Industry." Stanford, California: Stanford Research Institute, 1960.)

aftermath of nuclear catastrophe. "The tin hat and the sand bucket of World War II air raid wardens," the report argued, "must now be replaced by strange, new techniques for sheltering and shielding against enormous blast and heat and death-dealing rays that spread over the land with blowing winds." It was essential for civil defense organizations to "learn how to recover from the terrific impact of a nuclear assault, not only to tend the sick and wounded and keep life going, but to maintain essential production, and work toward full restoration of the economy."[1]

This was not the first time that the management of the critical infrastructures and industrial systems that comprise modern economies had been taken up as a central concern of military planning. In Europe and the United States, World War I had been a watershed for state-

---

1 Civil Defense for National Survival. Report of the House Committee on Government Operations. Washington, DC: US Government Printing Office, 1956 (hereafter, CDNS), p. 16.

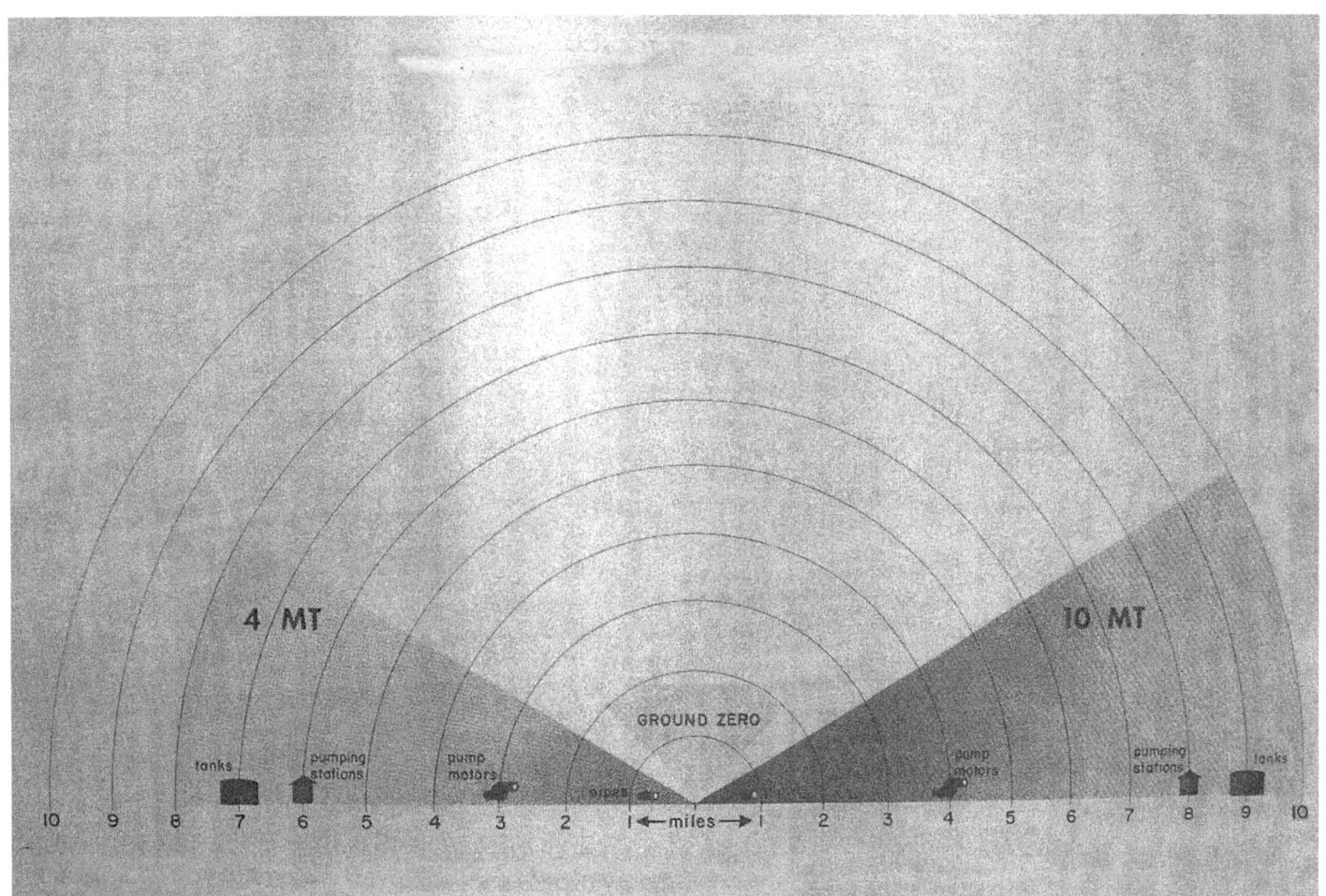

DAMAGE ESTIMATE
Radius of severe damage to pipeline components. (From Sanford B. Thayer and Willis W. Shaner, "Effects of Nuclear Attacks on the Petroleum Industry." Stanford, California: Stanford Research Institute, 1960.)

based economic planning in the interest of war mobilization. And in the United States, the War Production Board during World War II and the Office of Defense Mobilization during the Korean War invented various techniques of economic intervention as part of war mobilization efforts. In these agencies, war planners drew on new technical methods such as linear programming and matrix algebra to model the US economy as a complex of interdependent "activities" and to rationalize the allocation of scarce resources among competing priorities.

But this new stage of the Cold War led to a modulation of existing approaches to mobilization. Conventional war planning had focused on the *optimization* of the economy for war production. The thermonuclear age, by contrast, called for attention to economic *vulnerability*

to nuclear attack and to national survival in its aftermath. The problem of vulnerability, strategists argued, would require the invention of new methods of economic management. As William Stead, a consultant who conducted a study on non-military defense for the National Planning Association, testified: in the wake of nuclear war government officials would be "likely to be working with a severely damaged economy." It was necessary to "learn how to manage that damaged economy…to continue the essential industrial production and make preparation to do so."[2]

The experts and government officials who testified at the Hearings were preoccupied with gaps in the knowledge that would be required to manage the economy after a nuclear attack. Consider, for example, the testimony of Arthur Flemming, the head of the Office of Defense Mobilization—the organization most centrally involved in planning for national survival in the mid-1950s. Flemming told the Committee, "we are concerned over the lack of basic information [about] those items essential to survival following a bomb attack. All of those items … must be planned for in advance, requirements determined, stockpiles built up if necessary, and

vulnerability to attack lessened to the extent possible."[3] The existing knowledge practices of mobilization planning provided a starting point. On the basis of information collected by the Department of Commerce, the Department of the Interior, and the Census Bureau, ODM had recorded on computer tapes a vast amount of information about the US economy and population: "the precise location, shipments and employment of approximately 20,000 manufacturing plants in target areas; the 400 largest electric power generating stations; producers of the most important military end items and the principal elements and components and subassemblies of these items; principal airfields and military supply depots; the stockpile of strategic materials; and the United States population in 25,000 locations."[4] Using the new technical possibilities of "electronic calculators" like the Univac computer mobilization planners were able to assess the vulnerability of individual assets to nuclear detonations.[5] ODM led an interagency program that was "responsible for developing and maintaining a system for the assessment and reporting of attack damage and the impact of various patterns of attack on all segments of the mobilization base, including industry, man-

2 CDNS p. 1080.

3 Seventh Annual Report of the Activities of the Joint Committee on Defense Production. January 16, 1958. Washington: US Government Printing Office, p. 7-8.

4 CDNS, p. 1040.

5 CDNS, p. 1040.

power, telecommunication, transportation, and other mobilization resources".[6] This damage assessment center, equipped with powerful electronic computing equipment, was used to plan "hypothetical attacks against many targets in the United States and to compute the overall physical damage, radiological contamination, and casualties that can be expected".[7]

But this approach had shortcomings. It did not address the *systemic* effects that the disruption of individual elements could produce. "So far," Flemming reported, "we have been able to estimate physical destruction to productive facilities but not the effect on actual production, because of the complex chain of suppliers and subcontractors necessary to produce the finished product." In the future, ODM planned to record on tapes "information regarding this chain of production for selected critical weapons systems and survival requirements so that we will have a much clearer picture of our actual postattack production capability."

The crucial idea articulated here by Flemming is that production systems had properties that could not be understood by looking at the simple aggregation of their parts. Rather, one had to analyze the interconnections among these systems. Here, in the space between an isolated economic activity (such as the assembly of warships or airplanes in a specific factory) and a "chain of production"—between damage to individual facilities and *systemic* effects – we can see the emergence of a new way of thinking about and managing the US economy in the wake of a nuclear catastrophe.

Another expert who testified at the Hearings, operations analyst Walmer E. Strope of the Naval Radiological Defense Laboratory, described how one might use information about the vulnerability of industrial systems to plan for national survival in the wake of attack.[8] Strope described a hypothetical case of a dry-dock for ship repair that could withstand fifty pounds per square inch of blast pressure from a nuclear detonation, but that depended on a nearby power plant that was rated to only five psi. The greater protection of the dry-dock was "useless," he reasoned, "when the power plant would be destroyed." This type of "weak-link" analysis could be applied "not only to the plant or installation, but to the whole target area, and ultimately to the whole nation."[7] And indeed, over the course of the late 1950s and early 1960s, a number of government agencies as well as think tanks began to produce knowledge about vulnerable systems on ever-larger scales.

For example, in 1960, under contract with Office of Civilian and Defense Mobilization (OCDM), the successor to ODM, the Stanford Research Institute completed a study on "The Effects of Nuclear Attack on the Petroleum Industry" that examined the national "petroleum pipeline system" as an "integrated network of pipes, pumps, working tanks and controls." The study assessed not only the "vulnerability of the separate components of this system but also the "effect on over-all system operation caused by the loss of one or more components," and the likely reciprocal effects on interrelated systems such as electricity production and distribution that would themselves be damaged in a nuclear attack.[9] The National Planning Association engaged in an even more exhaustive modeling procedure under a contract signed with OCDM— which was reorganized in 1961 and renamed the Office of Emergency Planning (OEP). The result of this effort was a computer program called PARM (Program Analysis for Resource Management), a massive system for modeling the effects of nuclear attack by analyzing thousands of interlinked economic activities that, together, comprised the entire US economy.[10]

By the early 1960s, a new form of knowledge about American economic and social life had been consolidated within the agencies charged with preparing for thermonuclear war. With the aim of mitigating the vulnerabilities of the nation's vital systems to sudden and catastrophic attack, strategic planners quantified and analyzed the interrelations among distinct economic activities. Such expertise in system vulnerability would have a long career, in domains ranging from natural disaster, to terrorist attack, to pandemic disease, to economic crisis. □

STEPHEN J. COLLIER is Assistant Professor at The New School's Graduate Program in International Affairs.

ANDREW LAKOFF is Associate Professor of Sociology, Anthropology and Communication at University of Southern California.

---

6 CDNS, p. 1040.

7 CDNS, p. 1040.

8 Thus, in reference to Strope's example, Civil Defense for National Survival noted that "[i]n principle the requirements do not differ as between civilian and military targets. Protection of the shipyard workforce and facilities in, say, Long Beach California, and protection of the resident population are part of the same problem" (CDNS, p. 19).

9 CDNS, p. 19.

10 Sanford B. Thayer and Willis W. Shaner, "Effects of Nuclear Attacks on the Petroleum Industry." Stanford, California: Stanford Research Institute, 1960.

11 See Onur Ozgöde, "Logistics of National Survival," Department of Sociology, Columbia University, 2008.

THE EMERGENCE OF SYSTEMIC FINANCIAL RISK

FROM STRUCTURAL ADJUSTMENT (BACK) TO VULNERABILITY REDUCTION

BY ONUR OZGÖDE

FROM THE EARLY 1980S, national financial systems began to play an increasingly important role in the creation and distribution of wealth in modern capitalist economies. This structural transformation was celebrated by macroeconomists and policymakers, known as monetarists and neo-liberals, as a crucial step toward achieving sustainable and long-term economic growth, free of periodic recessionary disruptions due to cyclical adjustments in the structure of the economy. While this reform strategy proved to be successful in terms of minimizing both the frequency and the disruptive effects of recessions, it has brought into being a pathology of its own in the form of systemic financial crises.[1] At this juncture, financial catastrophes manifested themselves as the most serious threat not only to financial and macro-economic stability, but to socio-economic prosperity as well. In response to this new governmental problem, systemic risk emerged as the key governmental concept that animated recent regulatory initiatives to prevent and mitigate such catastrophes in the future.

The term systemic risk was coined at the onset of the Latin American debt crisis of the early 1980s by William Cline, an international economist who was a senior fellow at the Institute for International Economics at the time. The Institute, now the Peterson Institute for International Economics, was founded in 1981.[2] Circa 1979-80, Fred Bergsten, then the Assistant Treasury Secretary for International Affairs in the Carter administration, developed the initial blueprints of the Institute in response to a call from the German Marshall Fund (GMF). Bergsten, who had been a collaborator of Cline's at the Brookings Institution in the mid-1970s, had coordinated American foreign economic policy as Henry Kissinger's assistant for international economic affairs at the National Security Council (NSC). By the end of the decade, he had established himself as a leading policymaker with an expertise in international economics. After securing a $4 million grant from GMF (more than half of GMF's total budget) with the support of George Schultz, Nixon's Treasury Secretary who would soon become the Secretary of State under Reagan, Bergsten became the Institute's first and only director.[3]

The inception of the idea of founding the Institute can be traced back to an academic article co-authored by Bergsten and Cline in 1976. In this piece, entitled "Increasing International Economic Interdependence," the authors warned that growing interdependence between national economies was making them more vulnerable to external events such as oil, food and raw materials price shocks. Because such irregular disturbances were having increasingly destabilizing effects on economies, they called for macroeconomic models that would incorporate the foreign sector in more meaningful and detailed ways (Bergsten and Cline 1976). Indeed, American political and economic power was confronted in this decade with extraordinary and unforeseeable challenges. The collapse of the Bretton Woods fixed exchange rate system in 1971 turned out to be a major destabilizing force on the global monetary system and was followed by repeated and sharp declines in the value of the dollar throughout the 1970s. The emergence of OPEC in 1965 and the following two oil shocks, the first in 1973 and the second in 1979, demonstrated the vulnerability of the US economy to energy shocks. In light of these events, the Institute's main agenda was to shape policymaking on international economic issues that affected US foreign policy and the economy. The Latin American debt crisis, in this context, was

Fred Bergsten
Ph.D. in Economics 1969
Fletcher School of
Law & Diplomacy, Tufts University
Position at the Petersen Institute:
• Founding Director (1981-)
Trajectory Leading to the Institute:
• Assistant to Henry Kissinger, National Security Council, (1969-71)
• Senior Fellow, Brookings Institution (1972-76)
• Assistant Treasury Secretary for International Affairs, (1977-81)
• Undersecretary of Treasury for Monetary Affairs (1980–81)
Other positions held while at the Institute: unknown

1 Former Chairman of the Federal Reserve Board Allan Greenspan's arguments in favor of financial deregulation and increased financial flexibility was probably one of the best exemplars of this position. See (Subcommittee on Telecommunications and Finance of the Committee on Energy and Commerce 1994; Greenspan 2005).

2 According to its website, Peterson Institute tied as the top think tank in the world in 2008 in a survey of more than 5,000 similar institutions in the world (http://www.lie.Com/institute/aboutiiecCfm).

3 Other actors crucial in this process were his two close friends: New York Fed President Anthony Solomon and the Chairman and CEO of Lehman Brothers Peter Peterson. While Peterson, who had worked with Bergsten in the White House as an assistant to Nixon on international economic affairs, became the founding President of the Board of Directors, Solomon assumed the chairmanship of the Board's Executive Committee. Richard Cooper, a former NSC consultant and the Undersecretary of State for Economic Affairs in the Carter administration, was chosen to direct the Advisory Committee. See the biographies of actors on the Institute's website (www.iie.com) and Fred Bergsten's 25th anniversary celebration essay (Bergsten 2006).

the Institute's first major opportunity to interject itself in a critical policy discussion in Washington (Bergsten 2006).

Cline's interest in sovereign debt was born out of his dissertation research on economic development in Brazil in the late 1960s.[4] For the United States Agency for International De-

---

Peter G. Peterson

MBA 1951
University of Chicago
Position at the Petersen Institute:
• Founding President of the Board of Directors (1981-)
Trajectory Leading to the Institute:
• Assistant to the President for International Economic Affairs (Nixon, 1971-72)
• Secretary of Commerce (1972-73)
• CEO and Chairman of Lehman Brothers (1973-84)
Other positions held while at the Institute:
• Chairman of Council on Foreign Relations (1985-2007)
• Chairman of the New York Fed's Board of Directors (2000-04)

---

velopment (USAID), he coauthored two papers, one in 1969 and the other in 1971, on debt servicing and rescheduling by LDCs. These reports focused on 17 countries (8 of which were Latin American), since these nations accounted for more than half of the total foreign assistance received from developed countries in the previous decade (in absolute terms) and 15 of which were among the top 20 in this category. Debt servicing problems by these countries had begun to become an increasingly common phenomenon since the mid-1950s.[5] USAID contracted Cline to develop a measure for the capacity of a sovereign to service international debt and thereby construct a composite early warning indicator for predicting difficulties in debt servicing. Cline

---

Anthony Solomon

Ph.D. in Economics 1949
Harvard University
Position at the Petersen Institute:
• Chairman of the Board's Executive Committee (1981-2005)
Trajectory Leading to the Institute:
• Deputy Assistant Secretary of State for Latin America (Kennedy, 1963-65)
• Assistant Secretary of State for Economic Affairs (Johnson, 1965-69)
• Undersecretary of the Treasury for Monetary Affairs (Carter, 1977-80)
• President of the New York Fed (1980-85)
Other positions held while at the Institute: unknown

---

applied a statistical technique called "discriminant analysis" on historical data on instances of debt servicing delinquencies by these countries.[6] He used the technique to determine which macroeconomic variables, such as debt servicing ratio (the ratio of debt service to exports) and the growth rate of exports, could be considered indicators with high predictive power (Frank and

Cline 1971:329; Frank and Cline 1969).

In this line of work, Cline was not only silent on the possibility of a sovereign debt default as the outcome of debt servicing difficulties, but had also failed to consider the catastrophic and systemic effects of such an objective potentiality. Regardless of whether systemic risk was or was not intelligible to Cline at this juncture, the reason why he did not problematize systemic risk was that the scale of debt accumulated by LDCs at the time was objectively not that great. The main obstacle ahead for the sovereigns' ability to accumulate excessive levels of debt was the structural properties of the Bretton Woods monetary system within which the debt had to be accumulated. Thanks to the strict safeguards and regulations based on the core principle of the system, namely the Gold Standard, sovereigns were forced to adjust their monetary and exchange rate policies automatically before debt accumulation reached critical levels. Because this mechanism of automatic adjustment was supposed to ensure that the overall debt level always stayed low enough so that insolvency would not be a serious risk to the system, it was normal for Cline to consider a sovereign default virtually impossible. In this system of correlation, debt problems were framed almost always as one of (il)liquidity where the debtor would simply restructure the terms of its debt obligations through relief negotiations with the lenders. The challenge confronting policymakers, thus, was not to prevent a catastrophic default, but to ensure that such renegotiations would not become institutionalized as a commonly accepted practice inherent to the practice of acquiring sovereign international debt.

When Cline revisited the problem a decade later and introduced the term systemic risk for the first time in his 1984 book *International Debt: Systemic Risk and Policy Response,* a likely sovereign default and its potentially catastrophic

consequences for both the American and global financial systems were at the forefront of his agenda. Cline's book was an extended version of a previous paper he had published in the spring of 1982, only a few months before Mexico's call for a moratorium on its debt payments. With its curious title "External Debt: System Vulnerability and Development", this paper not only anticipated Cline's articulation of systemic risk as a formal concept in the coming years. It also marked a shift in his focus on and analysis of sovereign debt as a problem.

In the midst of the concerns over the ability of developing nations to service international debt without defaulting, Cline asked whether the global financial system would collapse "if there were a shock to the system from an interruption in the servicing of debt by developing countries."[7] To answer this question, he first analyzed the historical aggregate trend in early warning indicators for creditworthiness and

---

William R. Cline

Ph.D. in Economics 1969
Yale University
Position at the Petersen Institute:
• Senior Fellow (1981-)
Trajectory Leading to the Institute:
• Deputy Director of Development and Trade Research, Office of the Assistant Secretary for International Affairs, US Treasury (Nixon, 1971-73)
• Senior Fellow, Brookings Institution (1973-81)
Other positions held while at the Institute:
• Deputy Managing Director and Chief Economist, Institute for International Finance (1996-2001)

---

debt servicing for all non-oil developing countries, including Mexico. While there was no sign of deterioration in servicing ability at the aggregate level, the same could not be said for Brazil and Mexico, the two largest individual holders of debt that had enough accumulated debt to affect the entire system. Under the scenario of normal economic growth, sustained export-import balance and stable oil prices, Cline's model did not predict any problems. However, under two other stress scenarios in which oil prices either rose or declined, his model did forecast debt servicing ratios to increase rapidly as the export performance of both countries were highly sensitive to fluctuations in oil prices (Cline 1982: 6-7). Neither of these two scenarios was soothing.

In the late 1960s and early 1970s, Cline had conceptualized debt servicing delinquencies primarily as a problem of liquidity and consequently had deployed a kind of analysis that was backward looking and correlational in its logic. But this risk assessment technique was no longer useful in a situation where not only was the scale

---

4 His dissertation was on the impact of land reform on the productivity of the agricultural sector in Brazil (Cline 1969).

5 In the 1960s, 11 of these countries had experienced severe debt servicing problems 21 times, and Cline's forecasts would reveal all 17 were likely to have recurring rescheduling problems by the early 1980s.

6 Discriminant analysis was initially developed in biological and behavioral sciences, i.e. eugenics, in the 1930s for classifying a set of observed phenomena into classificatory categories based on each observation's individual characteristics. Between the 1940s and the 1960s, it was applied to consumer finance for predicting the risk of credit and financing delinquencies. It was specifically developed for predicting the occurrence of regular and frequent abnormalities that are normally distributed. Interestingly enough, Edward Altman, a contemporary of Cline who is now a pioneer in financial counterparty risk management, was utilizing this technique around the same time for measuring the risk of a firm failing, which was by nature an irregular and infrequent tail risks that are not normally distrusted (Altman 1968: 591).

7 While a rise in oil prices would increase the costs of Brazilian exports, a fall would cause Mexico's oil-based export strategy to fail (Cline 1982:4).

of debt accumulated within the system much greater, but also the structural properties of the system in which debt was accumulated constituted an environment of irreducible uncertainty for the lenders. In the world of post-Bretton Woods, there were neither set limits to the accumulation of sovereign debt nor an automatic

Richard Cooper
Ph.D. in Economics 1962
Harvard University
Position at the Petersen Institute:
• Chairman of the Advisory Committee (1981-)
Trajectory Leading to the Institute:
• Senior Staff Economist, Council of Economic Advisors (Kennedy, 1961-63)
• Harvard Economics (1965-66)
• Consultant to National Security Council (Early 1970s)
• Undersecretary of State for Economic Affairs (Carter, 1977-81)
Other positions held while at the Institute:
• Chairman of Boston Fed (1990-92)
• Chairman of National Intelligence Council (1995-97)

adjustment mechanism similar to the Gold Standard. Moreover, sovereign debt was mistakenly discounted as "riskless" by almost all major lender American mega-banks. The combination of these factors meant that a single instance of a debt servicing problem in one of these two countries would be enough to trigger a cascade of sovereign defaults in Latin America and undoubtedly result in bringing down a significant portion of the American banking system.

Confronted with these transformations in the nature of the problem, Cline adopted a distinct form of analysis of financial crisis that was forward looking and analytical in its logic. At the core of this analysis was an analytical technique called vulnerability assessment. Just as in an "analysis of strategic defense," this technique was deployed for assessing the effectiveness of "[a] system's defense mechanisms" against an external event that was unpredictable and unpreventable. Rather than measuring the expected increase in the marginal probability of the occurrence of an event, i.e. an instance of delinquency in debt servicing, in the form of a calculable risk, vulnerability assessment constituted the structural vulnerability accumulated within a system as an object of governmental intervention and thereby tried to measure it as a function of the system's ability to survive the impact of a shock originating from such an event. The key objective in this form of analysis, thus, was the reduction of the system's vulnerability to an external and unpreventable financial shock that was likely to be triggered by a sovereign default in Latin America. The American banking system's vulnerability had to be assessed and the

system's resilience increased to sufficient levels so that the system was robust enough to absorb and survive such a shock.

Cline conducted vulnerability assessment based on two factors: the sheer size of debt held by the debtor countries and the exposure of commercial banks to these countries. While the nine largest US banks had an exposure of 227.7 percent of their capital to these countries in 1981, 80 percent of this exposure was to Brazil and Mexico. Thus, a default by either would wipe out one-fifth of the large banks' capital, cause major liquidity problems, and force at least some into insolvency.[8] Although Cline had identified bank exposure to be the source of vulnerability, a year later in his 1983 study he added bank leverage as the final factor of vulnerability. While the size of debt and the extent of exposure put the banking system at risk, the highly leveraged structure of the American banking sector in general meant that a collapse in one part of the system would cause a contagion and severely affect the entirety of the American financial system.

In this respect, Cline's conceptualization of systemic risk can be considered to be a constitutive moment from a genealogical perspective. Admittedly, it was simply too early for Cline to be able to indentify the source of vulnerability as the system's high degree of interconnectedness in addition to the degree of leveraging within the system—as it has become clear with the financial crisis of 2008-9. Yet, to his credit Cline had realized that high leverage was enough to constitute certain clusters of banks as intrinsically vulnerable nodes within the system, which meant that the vulnerability of these nodes could be realistically characterized and analyzed without any reference to a specific external event. In the case of a failure in one or two critical nodes, a series of cascading failures could unfold within the banking system and cause a disruption in the flow of credit into the real economy. While Glass-Steagall's firewalls between different parts of the financial system could prevent the contagion from spreading from the banking system into other parts of the financial system, the failure of the banking system would be enough to instigate a deep recession, if not a full-blown depression.[9]

When the Latin American debt crisis finally came to a conclusion by the end of the 1980s, the problem of systemic risk was no longer at the forefront of the policy discussions on how to prevent a similar crisis in the future. In its stead, an alternative set of market-based policies gained currency under the banner of "Washington consensus." At the expense of Cline's structural vulnerability approach, this alternative programme of government intervention prioritized preventing the occurrence of external shocks through structural adjustment policies. These policies blamed governments for the structural distortions and market failures in the economy and thereby placed the burden of managing financial risks squarely on the shoulders of economic actors in financial markets (Williamson 1990; Williamson et.al. 1990). The financial crisis of 2008-9, however, revealed the limits of this preventative strategy of economic government. It proved that financial shocks were unpredictable and therefore unpreventable and that an exclusive focus on structural distortions and market failure was not sufficient to prevent such a crisis. Most importantly, it demonstrated the inability of economic actors to manage systemic risks that stem from structural vulnerabilities in a system. It is, thus, critical to recognize structural

John Williamson
Ph.D. in Economics 1963
Princeton University
Position at the Petersen Institute:
• Senior Fellow (1981-)
Trajectory Leading to the Institute:
• Economic Consultant to the UK Treasury (1968-70)
• Advisor to the IMF (1972-74)
• Various Academic Positions (1974-81)
Other positions held while at the Institute:
• Chief Economist for South East Asia at the World Bank (1996-99)

vulnerability as a distinct form of economic pathology and constitute it as the object of government intervention and regulation in order to ensure the resilience of the economy and the financial system against low probability and high impact shocks. The failure to do so will only lay the groundwork for more intense and frequent systemic financial crises in the future.□

ONUR OZGÖDE is a PhD candidate in Sociology at Columbia University.

---

8 The total exposure of the system was 151.1 percent in 1981. In 1977, it was 131.6 and 188.2 percent for the entire system and the largest nine banks respectively (Cline 1982: 9).

9 Under normal conditions what would be considered a benign piece of bad news could trigger a panic in bond markets that the overly indebted Latin American sovereigns were dependent on for financing their debt obligations. As the panic would quickly turn into a run on both the debt and the currencies of these countries, a series of sovereign defaults would ensue (Cline 1984).

UNCERTAIN ABOUT RISK

BY DOUGLAS R. HOLMES

IN JUNE 2010 I WAS IN LONDON talking to an official of the Bank of England. We were discussing a chart that projected GDP for the UK economy over the ensuing two years. It also happened to retrace the history of GDP since 2006 depicting the scale of the economic decline that marked the onset of the crisis. The chart, a "fan chart," is unusual insofar as it portrays graphically a probabilistic forecast of GDP with darker bands representing the more likely central projections of and lighter bands representing statistically less likely outcomes. Central banks are proud of their fan charts because they communicate transparently how their policy stance is intended to influence the economic activity over time as well as the limitations inherent in the forecasting exercise. That said, it was hard not be impressed with how this simple chart summarized the course of an astoundingly complex historical event.

We were discussing the uncertainties about evaluating recovery in the UK going forward when my interlocutor made a small observation about the chart. He noted that the fan chart projected backwards, that is it also depicted the past and present probabilistically. In other words, the scale of the downturn and the then current state of the UK recovery were far from clear in June 2010 and both could only be expressed probabilistically. The dimensions of the crisis we were living through were, thus, only understood imprecisely.

Representations of the economy—despite our obsessions with rendering them in exact mathematical terms—are fragile cultural constructions. My interlocutor's aside reminded me that an anthropological question resided in this chart, one that animated my research. He reminded me that the personnel of central banks while seeking to address pragmatic issues of monetary policy were engaged in a deep anthropology, a deep engagement with the representational forms—the models—that mediate our economic predicaments (Riles 2004).

The central bankers I study are preoccupied with monetary policy, the regulation of money and credit to the banking system. They are acutely aware of how uncertainty impinges on every aspect of their work. Their colleagues, who work in the financial stability divisions, are the figures centrally concerned with systemic risk. In the midst of the financial tumult that commenced in September 2008, these two central bank operations increasingly converged.

In the brief, telegraphic comments that follow, I look at how the problems addressing uncertainty intersect with the predicaments posed by systemic risk. What I am trying to do is to see if I can establish a premise, a starting point for

Percentage increases in output on a year earlier

Bank estimates of past growth   Projection

ONS data

2006 07 08 09 10 11 12 13

AUGUST 2010 ESTIMATE Bank of England's fan chart, estimating of Gross Domestic Product.

(ONS is The Office for National Statistics, the UK Government's single largest statistical producer.)

ethnographic inquiry into reciprocal relationship between uncertainty and risk under the sway of performativity. What is revealed in this exercise is the way ethnography can be designed to pursue inquiry under conditions of radical indeterminacy.[1]

THE DISTINCTION

The definition of "systemic risk" outlined in Wikipedia provides a good starting point: "It refers to the risks imposed by interlinkages and interdependencies in a system or market, where the failure of a single entity or cluster of entities can cause a cascading failure, which could potentially bankrupt or bring down the entire system or market" (http://en.wikipedia.org/wiki/Systemic_risk, accessed November 20, 2010).

Frank Knight formulated the classic distinction between risk and uncertainty. Here is Knight's delineation of the two concepts.

Uncertainty must be taken in a sense radically distinct from the familiar notion of Risk, from which it has never been properly separated.... The essential fact is that 'risk' means in some cases a quantity susceptible of measurement, while at other times it is something distinctly not of this character; and there are far-reaching and crucial differences in the bearings of the phenomena depending on which of the two is really present and operating… It will appear that a measurable uncertainty, or 'risk' proper, as we shall use the term, is so far different from an unmeasurable one that it is not in effect an uncertainty at all (Knight 1921:19-20).

The practical difference between the two categories, risk and uncertainty, is that the former the distribution of the outcome in a group of instances is known (either through calculation a priori or from statistics of past experience), while in the case of uncertainty this is not true, the reason being in general that it is impossible to form a group

of instances, because the situation dealt with is in a high degree unique (Knight 1921: 233).

Life is mostly made up of uncertainties, and the conditions under which an error or loss in one case may be compensated by other cases are bafflingly complex. We can only say that "in so far as" one confronts a situation involving uncertainty and deals with it on its merits as an isolated case, it is a matter of practical indifference whether the uncertainty is measurable or not (Knight 1921: 235).

The efforts to erase this distinction created the intellectual foundations for the current financial crisis.

In a remarkable, unpublished paper by Stephen Nelson and Peter Katzenstein entitled, "Uncertainty and Risk and the Crisis of 2008," the authors trace out how rationalist approaches in economics—deeply committed to sophisticated mathematical modeling—sought to treat uncertainty as a species of calculable risk. They note that John von Neumann and Oskar Morgenstern (1947) provided economists with a sophisticated means to model rational choice under conditions of risk and how this agenda transformed the discipline over the subsequent half century. I cannot do full justice to their account herein; it is intricate and persuasive analysis demonstrating how uncertainty was increasingly treated by academics as calculable risk and why this was so compelling to economists and to bankers. What they further demonstrate is how this profound intellectual error punctuated just about every aspect of crisis that we are currently living through. Donald Mackenzie examines in *An Engine, Not a Camera: How Financial Models Shape Markets* these issues in relation to the Black-Scholes-Merton equation. Basically the same maneuver of relentlessly quantifying risk while eliminating uncertainty was, as he demonstrates, at the center of Long-Term Capital's debacle presaging many aspects of the current

1 The discussion that forms the second part of this essay was developed initially in longer piece entitled, "Economy of words" (Holmes 2009).

crisis providing vectors of contagion across the financial system.

PERFORMATIVITY REGIME

Here is where the story becomes particularly vertiginous. Economists believed during the last half of the twentieth century that they were embarked on an enterprise to make economics increasingly precise, predictive, and, thus, scientific. The value of their methodological innovations, modeled on physics, is of course open to debate (MacKenzie 2001; Samuelson 1947).

Good empirical evidence tells its story regardless of the precise way in which it is analyzed. In large part it is its simplicity that makes it persuasive. Physicists do not compete to find more elaborate ways to observe falling apples. Instead they have made progress because theory has sought inspiration from a wide range of empirical phenomena. Macroeconomics could progress in the same way. But progress is unlikely as long as macroeconomists require the armor of a stochastic pseudoworld before doing battle with evidence from the real one. (Summers 1991:146)

What economists did succeed at and what is not debatable is that they created a "performative" regime by which their ideas, their theories, their models were assimilated by experts (as if they were true and valid) and designed into the intellectual structure of contemporary institutions. Economic ideas were put at the service of making reality not merely representing it analytically.

Michel Callon...proposed elucidating explicitly the performative character of economics; that is, he proposes considering economics not as a form of knowledge that depicts an already existing state of affairs but as a set of instruments and practices that contribute to the construction of economic settings, actors, and institutions... (MacKenzie, Muniesa, & Siu 2007: 3-4).

Thus, treating uncertainty as calculable risk was not a matter of a flawed academic exercise or experiment, rather as these assumptions were engineered directly into the models employed to manage and to regulate the system, they themselves became the sources of contagion and the motors of systemic risk. In other words, it was not merely that academics got the story wrong, not merely that their formal analytical models were responsible for grotesque misrepresentations of workings of markets; rather, it was how these models came to be built into the working of the financial system—secreted deep in its regulatory frameworks—and, thus, how these ideas became fully implicated in the ensuing destructive storm (Riles 2001, 2010).

BETWEEN THE CUP AND LIP

The other great theorist of uncertainty is, of course, J. M. Keynes, who stated his position in a famous, lyrical passage in the *General Theory of Employment, Interest, and Money.*

We have now introduced money into our causal nexus for the first time, and we are able to catch a first glimpse of the way in which changes in the quantity of money work their way into the economic system. If, however, we are tempted to assert that money is the drink which stimulates the system to activity, we must remind ourselves that there may be several slips between the cup and the lip. For whilst an increase in the quantity of money may be expected, ceteris paribus, to reduce the rate of interest, this will not happen if the liquidity-preferences of the public are increasing more than the quantity of money; and whilst a decline in the rate of interest may be expected, ceteris paribus, to increase the volume of investment, this will not happen if the schedule of the marginal efficiency of capital is falling more rapidly than the rate of interest; and whilst an increase in the volume of investment may be expected, ceteris paribus, to increase employment, this may not happen if the propensity to consume is falling off. Finally, if employment increases, prices will rise in a degree partly governed by the shapes of the physical supply functions, and partly by the liability of the wage-unit to rise in terms of money. And when output has increased and prices have risen, the effect of this on liquidity-preference will be to increase the quantity of money necessary to maintain a given rate of interest (Keynes 2007[1936]: 155).

For Keynes, the economy operated in our world, where *ceteris paribus* does not necessarily obtain, where the rational and the irrational co-exist or may be entirely inseparable, where knowledge is imperfect, and where information is asymmetrical, and experience and intuition can or must inform judgment (Holmes 2009, Zaloom 2004). The shifting and fugitive dynamics of global markets, their operation from innumerable perspectives is made available to us through the inter-mediation of language, through agile linguistic scenarios that are susceptible to continuous modification and elaboration (Lakoff and Johnson 1980; McCloskey 1985, 1990, 1994; Smart 1999, 2006).

Keynes' evocative accounts yielded an analytical tableau—in many respects congruent with an ethnographic framework—to be communicated to a public, an elite public of politicians, bankers, academics, businessmen, and journalists who populated his analytic landscape thus making its features susceptible to policy interventions, to persuasion. Uncertainty had to be addressed at every turn, calculable risk was elusive and capricious.

The possibilities and limitations of economic method and theory were predicated on particular historical circumstances. Keynes insinuated on to this landscape protagonists capable of thinking and acting critically within and upon the then contemporary world. Keynes sought not merely to debate, to persuade, and to otherwise influence these subjects, but learn from them. "The economist's task was to discern the form or style suitable to the age—a matter of aesthetics and logic...Keynes always stressed the crucial importance of "vigilant observations" for successful theory-construction—theory being nothing more, in this view, than stylized reorientation of the dominant tendencies of the time, derived from reflection on the salient facts" (Skidelsky 1992:221).

I have developed the notion of an "economy of words" to encompass the means for modeling linguistically and, hence, communicatively economic phenomena operating at the limits of calculation and measurement (Holmes 2009). In this economy "at large" or "in the wild," as Michel Callon (2007) describes it, words perform the decisive function of creating context—countless contexts—that frame data series, statistical measures, and econometric projections. The shifting and fugitive dynamics of global markets, their operation from innumerable perspectives is made available to us through the inter-mediation of language, through agile linguistic scenarios that are susceptible to continuous modification and elaboration. The narrative practices pursued by central bankers are by no means indifferent or antagonistic to the realm of numbers, far from it; in the first instance they are shaped by the analytical predicaments posed by various forms of statistical measurement and quantitative analysis. Indeed, words are continually employed to scrutinize the nature of economic categories and the vagaries of statistical measurement (Blinder et al 2001). In my broader project I argue that through the construction of acute "econometric scenarios" central bankers create the economy itself as a communicative field and empirical fact. At every turn these scenarios are underwritten by uncertainties that encompass incalculable risks. □

DOUGLAS R. HOLMES *is professor of anthropology at Binghamton University.*

THE CYBER-BEHAVIORIST ORIGINS OF
SOFT TORTURE

BY REBECCA LEMOV

AT THE MACY FOUNDATION CONFERENCE on cybernetics in 1951 the inveterate inventor of information theory, Claude Shannon, shocked an assembled crowd when he debuted an electronic rat he had built. (I use the word "debut" advisedly, for this event really did resemble a theatrical debut.) Set down at the opening of a metallic grid that held a five-foot square walled maze, Shannon's diminutive automaton, fondly christened "Rat," proceeded to work its way through to the end. Although its movements were not smooth or graceful, and although it looked nothing like an actual maze-navigating rodent, it performed with something like aplomb. When at last it hit the "goal," a designated sensor on the grid, it lit itself up, rang a bell, and stopped its own motors, as if in celebration. "The machine has solved the maze," declared its inventor—who, just three years earlier, had authored for Bell Labs his *Mathematical Theory of Communication,* a work hailed by the end of the century as "the Magna Carta of the Information Age."

On that day, Rat riveted a crowd of twenty-five of the nation's foremost social, behavioral, and physical scientists. They had gathered for the eighth of ten meetings unified under the theme of "Circular and Causal Feedback Mechanisms in Biological and Social Systems." What had them on the edge of their seats was not just Rat's clever engineering. The maze-solving machine was in fact very simple, made of a "sensing finger" hooked up to two motors, one that operated in the east-west, the other in the north-south direction. By means of these components it could maneuver whatever configuration of the maze—for the structure had moveable walls—Shannon chose to arrange. What gripped the audience was a quality akin to pathos: rather than watching something (say, a highly trained lab rat) simply succeed automatically in solving a maze, the audience was watching it trying, failing, testing, going awry, and finally making its way. The electronic rat and maze were one system, and the system, in an "all too human" way (in the words of one onlooker), worked. Rat learned. This struck the assembled crowd as significant. It offered a model on which all kinds of social and biological systems could be based.

This was not all, though. Having electrified the crowd, Rat went on to unnerve it. Shannon's maze-solving machine had a second act. After Rat navigated the maze and rang its own chime, Shannon showed how easily it could fall into error. Shift a few variables, alter the parameters making the previous solution no longer tenable, and there it was running in circles in an endless loop from which it could never emerge without external input: it was stuck in a "vicious circle, … a singing condition," and all its purported "efforts" to alter its course only made it more stuck. Audience members reached for literary equivalents: psychiatrist Henry Brosin remarked, "George Orwell … should have seen this." "Psycho" Rat (as one participant called it) and Triumphalist Rat were alternatives, two possible futures. (Two decades earlier, certain behavioral experts, precursors to cybernetics and systems theory, had expressed just such warnings about seeking a science of control: the more successful you were, the more you had to reckon with the specter of "a wild and unadaptive chaos of behavior" that would spread should something go wrong.)

The same year as Rat performed its twin futures a new paradigm in the American behavioral sciences emerged called coercive persuasion—and, I argue, these two events shared a common genesis in theories of systems. Coercive persuasion was the U.S. scientific response to the political-intellectual crisis about communist brainwashing capabilities that in the early 1950s gripped high-up levels of government and quickly spread through popular audiences. U.S. Air Force pilots appeared in newsreel footage blaming imperialism and admitting to germ-warfare missions; twenty-one American GI's held as Korean War POWs defected to communist lands; and there appeared to be a blind spot in American individualism, which was evidently vulnerable to *Manchurian-Candidate*-style ideological engineering.

A fleet of behavioral scientists took on the task of studying this phenomenon, this "something new in history," as writer Eugene Kinkead for the *New Yorker* ominously called it. They argued somewhat contradictorily if self-servingly that brainwashing did not exist (there was no hocus-pocus, magical way to psychologically extinguish a human being) and that, even if it did, it was not what you thought it was. Brainwashing was really nothing more than sophisticated behaviorism, the kind of thing done to rats in mazes for decades. The resulting science of coercive persuasion, sometimes also known as "forceful interrogation," was based on viewing the prisoner within his situation as a single system, much as Rat in his electronic maze made up a system. No longer was the prisoner seen primarily as an individual exerting heroic effort—or failing mightily—against forces that threatened to break him down into a dehumanized shell of his former self. Instead, a systems approach to coercion viewed the individual-within-the-environment as a set of circulating messages. The environment could be changed—made colder or hotter, smaller or larger, louder or quieter, more or less stimulating, more or less humiliating—and the subject, like Shannon's Rat in his ever-changing electronic maze, would surely reflect these changes, acting in turn on the environment. At last, the subject was no longer the sole possessor of his own internal life; rather, in effect, his internal life was a product of external relationships, and it existed somewhere in the interaction of self and surroundings. To put it baldly, the self was now an epiphenomenon, a mere part of an information system.

As one researcher (Dr. Robert Jay Lifton) reported, "milieu control," the first and most powerful technique to bring about thought reform in a target, entailed foremost the fine-tuned control and circulation of messages. Another (Donald Hebb) found that sensory deprivation, brought about when environmental surroundings were completely controlled by being blocked, resulted in extreme changes in experimental subjects in very short periods of time—within hours. The inner states of such experimental subjects were no longer envisioned as "inside," but were seen as complex information networks. After all, if a matter of a few hours in a sensory deprivation tank could result in extreme dissociation, what did this say about the autonomy of the human self? An additional behavioral expert (Dr. Louis Jolyon West) found that a process of amounting to extreme environmental manipulation had led to what was sometimes called the "ultimate demoralization" of imprisoned men: as his research team

IT'S A RAT RACE
Claude Shannon debuts his
electro-mechanical rat.

reported, "Whenever individuals show extremely selective responsiveness to only a few situational elements, or become generally unresponsive, there is a disruption of the orderliness, i.e., sequence and arrangement of experienced events, the process underlying time spanning and long-term perspective." The result was a tragedy for the prisoner, but a research boon for the systems theorist: "By disorganizing the perception of those experiential continuities constituting the self-concept and impoverishing the basis for judging self-consistency, [extreme environmental control] affects one's habitual ways of looking at and dealing with oneself." When treated as information, even the self could be scrambled.

This flood of new research—on systemic demoralization—marked the arrival of cybernetics, information theory, and systems theory within projects that would previously have stood firmly in one camp, be it the conduct of war or the pursuit of basic stimulus-response psychology. During the post-World War II years, new fields not only spoke to each other, they frenziedly traded once-trademarked techniques, piggybacking on and adding to each others' special methods; they reached across once respected aisles. It amounted to a new way of viewing what it meant to be human: now, according to brainwashing experts influenced by systems theory, the human subject was something akin to information distributed within a milieu. As mentioned above, the human being (prisoner, subject, spy) within a controlled environment (prison, reeducation camp, barracks) was no longer seen as an individual involved in a meaningful struggle. Rather, according to a cybernetic approach to "biological and social systems," he was information that circulated within a system. According to prominent psychologist James A. Miller, avatar of a general behavior systems theory, systems are "bounded regions in space-time, involving energy interchange among their parts, which are associated in functional relationships, and with their environments." Instead of a vision of a complex, Freudian, deep, singular self, behavioral scientists like Miller described a distributed set of relationships, ever changing, responding to new conditions and new information. Beyond that, in many cases, lay a fantasy of complete, push-button control over each designated Rat and every potential POW, over ideological enemies, spies, deviants, and even consumers. At the same time, the more

experts sought systemic control, the more the system was at risk of chaotic outbursts, "singing conditions," and unpredictable instability.

All told, in the postwar world, a systems approach enabled researchers to fathom what had happened, to protect against it happening to American G.I.s (it was hoped), and to engineer its use against the enemy. So emerged a program in what has been called "soft torture": the thoroughgoing use of environmental input—manipulation of the prisoner's sleep, temperature, clothing, body image, anxiety level, sense of dignity and ultimately sense of self—to bring about demoralization and to extract "actionable intelligence." (Whether "good" intelligence ever emerges from such scenarios is a matter of much debate; experienced interrogators say such information is never useful.)

During the post-9/11 campaigns in Afghanistan and Iraq, these techniques reemerged, in a story that has been well told. Then Abu Ghraib happened. Abu Ghraib showed what occurs when systems of milieu control involving variables of complexity hit a glitch. It is interesting to note, however, that subsequent debate in the American public sphere was not about sophisticated interrogation procedures involving advanced environmental engineering and the combination of techniques, nor about the massive *regularization and standardization* of what amounted to torture—for by this point some 21,000 interrogations had been routinely performed under exacting bureaucratic standards. Instead the debate ended up revolving around whether "a few bad apples" on the one hand, or Donald Rumsfeld on the other, were to blame. By 2004, passions had come to settle on a single, spectacular technique, waterboarding. This ignored the fact that such coercion happens as part of a system (whether or not it ends up getting 'actionable results'), and systems include within their workings the threat of behavior chaos, indeed rely on it. But unlike Rat performing in his electronic maze, which to an expert audience once clearly dramatized a vision of possible futures, most onlookers today are still not interested in seeing this. □

REBECCA LEMOV *is at Harvard University.*

THE PRE-HISTORY OF RESILIENCE IN ECOLOGICAL RESEARCH

BY BRIAN LINDSETH

The notion of resilience has become increasingly salient in recent decades in fields ranging from public health preparedness to critical infrastructure protection. As Benjamin Sims has noted in this issue of LIMN, the use of the concept of resilience to indicate a norm that critical systems should strive for comes from the field of systems ecology – specifically from a seminal 1973 article by C.S. Holling. In *Brittle Power,* Amory and L. Hunter Lovins provide a key example in their call to "formulate the principles of a design science of resilience." They attribute their debt to those "who study the survival and stability of ecosystems," and particularly "the Canadian Ecologist Professor C.S. Holling."[1] In this essay I explore the meaning and intellectual lineage of Holling's concept of resilience.

---

1 Lovins and Lovins (1983: 174, 182).

IN HIS 1973 ARTICLE, Holling contrasts approaches emphasizing the dynamism, complexity, and unpredictability of nature with a more widespread view emphasizing the stability of nature.[2] In foregrounding a comparatively narrow range of relations between populations of predators and prey, the latter approach overemphasizes the durability of supposedly stable equilibrium relations and obscures other kinds of relations. By contrast, an approach based on resilience is more open to the dynamism and complexity of the natural world. This openness allows ecologists to recognize the systems in nature that can survive disturbances, if often in different forms.

In addition to this emphasis on dynamism and complexity, his article is striking for the degree of abstraction with which it describes phenomena in nature. Instead of details about

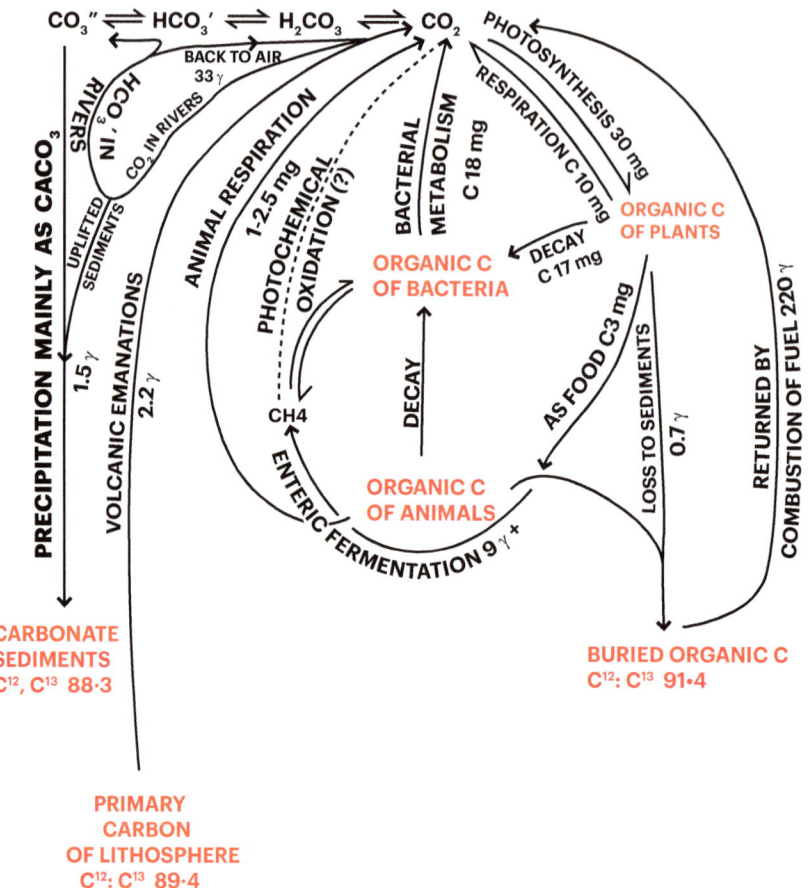

THE CARBON CYCLE (after Hutchinson 1948: 228)

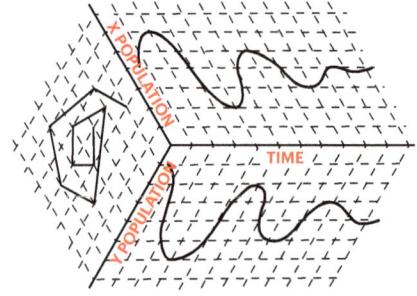

DERIVATION OF A PHASE PLANE Showing the changes in numbers of two populations over time (after Holling 1973: 3).

populations of plants or animals at a specific field site, the reader encounters hypothetical models of predator prey relations represented as "trajectories in the phase plane."[3] Although its attack on equilibrium-based approaches occupies the core of Holling's argument, underlying this argument was the assumption that the world is a place made up of abstract systems. Where did this notion come from and how did it occupy the place of an assumption in Holling's article?

In order to answer this question, we need to examine the formation of systems ecology as the milieu from which Holling's article emerged. Materializing in the mid-to-late 1960s, systems ecology is known for fusing an inclusive, holistic approach with a comparatively

intensive reliance on mathematics and the use of computers to model ecosystem dynamics in all of their complexity. In noting that training in mathematics and biomathematics would help ecologists move more easily "across the gap that separates the real world from the world of mathematical abstraction," systems ecologist Kenneth Watt drew attention to one of the core features of this form of ecological research—its reliance on abstraction to describe key processes in nature.[4] While these ecologists would puzzle over questions such as how many of nature's variables to include in their models of a given system, the notion that nature was a place composed of systems was something that was no longer discussed as it had become an assumption accord-

ing to which research in systems ecology made sense.

The formation of this field—along with its central assumption, that nature is made up of systems—would be an important condition of possibility for Holling's notion of resilience. As ecologists reached for the language and tools of cybernetics in the late 1940s and systems analysis in the 1960s, they would also define nature in the increasingly abstract language of systems. In these two moments we can see an early and somewhat tentative search for systems *in* nature culminate in the assumption that nature itself was *made up of* systems. The relevance of the history of the field to Holling's 1973 article runs deeper, however. In addition to this form

---

2 Holling has more recently characterized the latter as part of an engineering perspective (Sims, this issue, p. 6).

3 Holling (1973: 3).

4 Watt (1966b: 266). See also the call of fellow systems ecologist Bernard Patten (1966: 593).

of systems-based abstraction, Holling's article also bears the mark of the field's early efforts to define itself against population ecology in its emphasis on dynamism and complexity.

In drawing on the language of cybernetics, ecologist G. Evelyn Hutchinson's description of the cycles by which matter moves through the environment as self-regulating represents an early effort to find systems in nature. He depicted these 'circular causal systems' in a talk that was delivered at a New York Academy of Science conference on cybernetics that took place immediately after the second Macy Conference in 1946.[5] Faced with a variety of cycles of different kinds of elements often in different settings, Hutchinson isolated and described the key ecological process shared despite all of these differences. Further, he did it using the same vocabulary other conference participants were applying to a proliferating array of problems.[6]

IF HUTCHINSON'S USE of cybernetics represents one key moment in the pre-history of Holling's article, another is the more proximal formation of systems ecology in the 1960s. Kenneth Watt was one of the key figures in clearing the space for systems ecology in this period. In 1962 he published an article attacking the models used in population ecology as overly simplistic and reflective of a disjuncture between theory and empirical observation.[7] A distinctive feature of Watt's attack is the extent to which it emerged from an area of ecology that had much in common with population ecology. Both areas relied on mathematical modeling to abstract processes from nature, and the process of interest for systems ecology would be the same as that for population ecology—relations between populations of predators and prey. From this perspective, we can see Watt's attack as doing the work of defining systems ecology in contrast with the more established field of population ecology. The models of population ecology were too simple, he argued, and existed in a theoretical vacuum.[8]

Nonetheless, as a field defining itself as more inclusive but also reliant on complicated mathematical models, the prospect of modeling in a more inclusive way an object that was so complex represented a formidable challenge. The level of complexity (now methodological)

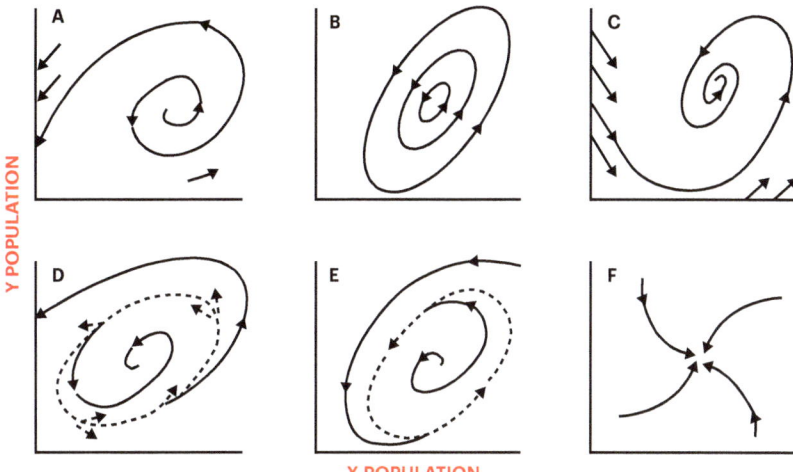

EXAMPLES OF POSSIBLE BEHAVIORS OF SYSTEMS IN A PHASE PLANE (a) unstable equilibrium, (b) neutrally stable cycles, (c) stable equilibrium, (d) domain of attraction, (e) stale limit cyle, (f) stable node. (After Holling 1973: 4)

introduced by stripping away the simplifying assumptions of population ecologists would prove intractable for the traditional tools of ecology. In a 1966 volume that served as a rallying cry for the emerging field of systems ecology, Kenneth Watt boldly answered this dilemma. Ecology should incorporate the tools of systems analysis as a field that is used to dealing with complexity. Ecologists should use computers to run simulations but also to process the increased number of mathematical equations coming from incorporating nature's complexity.[9]

In his contribution to Watt's 1966 volume, Holling shared Watt's interest in using the terms of systems analysis—of positive and negative feedback, computer simulation, and approaching key processes of interest as systems—to describe nature. The differences between the 1966 and 1973 articles are instructive, however. By 1973, Holling was no longer focused on making a case for systems analysis so much as basing a paradigm shift in the study of populations that presumed the value of the systems approach. He opened his 1966 essay by noting that in the face of the onslaughts of man, "nature has proved to be remarkably resilient."[10] In his 1973 article on resilience, he *assumes* the reader will similarly value a focal point centered on "the behavior of systems."[11] In this article it is the systems that make up nature that are resilient in the specific

sense that the article defines—not nature as he described it in 1966, in the language of an emerging environmental movement.

BY 1973, HUTCHINSON'S search for systems in nature had become the assumption that nature was a place made up of systems. This shift, a move towards abstraction and reliance on the vocabulary of systems, is a precondition of Holling's notion of resilience. Before a system could be more or less resilient, there first had to be the assumption that nature was made up of systems. Further, we can see the field's struggles of self-definition echoing forward into Holling's 1973 article. His attack on the emphasis on stability is also (following Watt) an attack on overly simplistic approaches in population ecology.

If, as I have suggested, understanding the milieu of Holling's 1973 article is an important step in understanding the notion of resilience, then its subsequent uptake by analysts interested in systemic risk suggests questions about the extent to which this more recent, less ecological milieu might have re-shaped resilience as a target of intervention. □

BRIAN LINDSETH *is a PhD candidate in Sociology at University of California, San Diego.*

5 Galison (1994) and Heims (1991) both describe the Macy Conferences as an important milieu in the formulation and extension of cybernetics. This particular meeting was organized by Lawrence Frank to take advantage of the fact that the Macy participants would be in New York at the time and included cybernetics luminaries such as Norbert Wiener and Warren McCulloch (Heims 1991: 80).

6 Heims (1991). Galison (1994) provides an account of the beginnings of cybernetics in the war time work of Norbert Wiener and its subsequent uptake in the postwar years.

7 To be sure, this was not a new criticism. The sub-field's reliance on the insights from outside the field of ecology—from the physical and social sciences but especially demography—was long the source of skepticism from the ecological mainstream. By the postwar period, however, population ecology had become firmly established area of research (Kingsland 1995).

8 See Palladino (1991) for more on the relation between systems ecology and population ecology.

9 Watt sums up this argument, "The central motive for using systems analysis in ecology is the complexity of ecological processes" (1966a: 5). He proceeds to note that "Simulation figures prominently in the arsenal of tricks used by systems analysts" (1966a: 5). In order to take advantage of systems analysis ecologists need more training in mathematics and biomathematics but also FORTRAN and systems analysis (1966b: 266). Interestingly, systems ecology would form what historian of ecology Paolo Palladino has characterized as "a paradoxical alliance" (Palladino 1991: 229) or a "shotgun marriage" (McIntosh 1988: 228) with ecosystem ecology.

10 Holling (1966: 195).

11 Holling (1973:1).

SYSTEMIC RISK IN CONSUMER FINANCE

BY MARTHA POON

At the end of the great credit bubble there was still a tremendous amount of borrowing potential in the hands of consumers. Of the $5 trillion in US credit card lines outstanding only $800 billion was reportedly in use. So in the spring of 2009, with unemployment and bankruptcy on the rise, the card companies started to purge their books of plastic. Lenders began unilaterally closing unused accounts in a furious attempt to control costs and reduce exposure. They also began 'balance chasing', the practice of systematically trimming down credit line limits as debts get paid off.

Suddenly, through no fault of their own, US consumers with strong credit ratings started seeing their scores slide down the chute. When a lender decided to close a card or cut a line, an individual's overall credit limit was lowered, and the ratio of line to limit use was instantly increased. This in turn lowered their FICO® credit bureau score, sometimes by more than 50 points. As lenders reabsorbed lines in the transition out of a credit soaked environment, the credit ratings these lines were supporting also deflated. What dropping FICO® scores indicated was this: as credit contracted, the credit risk within the system was increasing.

FICO® is not just an observation of credit risk. It is also a tool that is actively used to manage credit accounts. So the crushing involuntary landslide didn't stop at the scores. Following the fine print in card contracts, decreases in ratings triggered ballooning interest rates from as much as 7.99% to 28%, even on accounts where no action had occurred. Not only was less credit immediately available, but the affected consumers who had yet to default on a payment were now facing higher monthly payments on multiple cards, an accelerated accrual of debt, and a compromised position in the markets because of a weakened score.[1]

The process of credit contraction—initiated by financial institutions and propagated by plunging scores—has exposed FICO® as an important machinery of market feedback and control. FICO® mediates the risk management decisions of numerous independently acting firms whose collective activities feed into macroeconomic phenomena. What is the system of consumer finance? What are its constituent parts and how are they connected? The answer is through FICO®. The heart of consumer finance is a machine that produces trademarked risk information. What credit contraction shows is that the systemic quality of US consumer finance and the use of this information system are one and the same.

This raises the question of systemic risk. In finance, systemic risk has traditionally referred to the possibility that a loss incurred at one banking institution could propagate outwards, unleashing a chain of events through which the financial system as a whole would fail. Systemic risk should not be conflated with an economic downturn or dramatic losses[2] that are natural parts of what is at stake in financial activity. Rather it is concerned with the catastrophic loss of functioning in the system of finance itself, thought to be triggered by an event occurring within a single firm. (The classic trigger in this model is a bank run.)

The rise of global capital markets, however, complicates this picture. Within capital markets the number of actors at play proliferates to include alternative institutional intermediaries, financial instruments and transactional ties that fall outside of banking relationships. The nature of the system that is at risk becomes much more amorphous once its components are not limited to a discreet category of agents such as banks. The domino effect is overwhelming evidence of profound interconnectedness within capital markets. By the same token, however, the freeze has made systemic risk the object of regulatory scrutiny at precisely the moment when it is most difficult to map out the markets' heterogeneous parts.

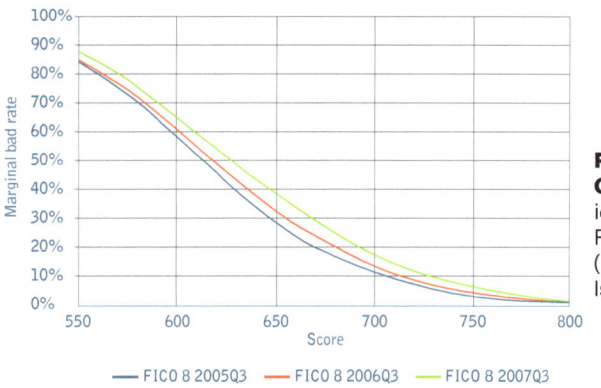

RATES HIGHER OVER TIME Economic Conditions drive FICO® 8 score bad. (Image ©2010 Fair Isaac Corporation)

I would like to draw attention to two observations raised by this contraction in order to parse out a relationship between 'system' and 'risk' that is significantly different from the one that is described by the traditional institution-based model of financial action and financial regulation. The first is that actionable risk in consumer credit markets is constituted within a material infrastructure for calculating credit scores. The risk of default is issued from this proprietary machinery and can only be seized and acted upon by agents interacting with this material apparatus. The second is that the routine exercise of the logic of risk versus return carried through the signs emitted by this machine creates instability at the macroeconomic level.

This suggests that FICO® should be considered a key location of political intervention. If systemic risk implies the threat of an event that could disrupt widespread consumer economic participation, and if risk scores are to play a pivotal role in how that event unfolds, then the way to manage systemic risk is to mitigate the trigger at the level of the risk assessment machine. The purpose of intervention would not be to treat any permanently resolvable flaw within FICO®. Rather intervention would address the fact that by its very capacity to coordinate widespread financial action, FICO® is capable of generating conditions that are crises from the point of view of lived experience and political objectives.

It is noteworthy that neither FICO® itself as a technical system, nor the logic of action it promotes are placed in jeopardy by the politicization of these conditions. As regulators embrace the concept of risk and identify the distributed effects of risk-based activity as the new objects of regulatory control, it is arguable that they are only promoting the historical transformation towards a greater preoccupation with risk that the invention of FICO® announces. Thus, I would argue, in finance the nature of systemic risk is shifting. It is no longer refers to the threat of widespread dysfunction posed by a single institution. It is now the effect of having engineered material systems for producing risk information that serve as contemporary organizational forms. □

MARTHA POON *is currently Visiting Scholar at the Institute for Public Knowledge, New York University.*

FICO® is the heart of consumer finance—a machine that produces trademarked risk information.

---

1 This was occurring prior to and in anticipation of the Credit Card Accountability, Responsibility, and Disclosure Act signed in May 22, 2009. The act outlawed universal default, the practice of changing the terms of a loan in function of an default occurring with another institution discovered through credit bureau information and/or credit score.

2 Schwarcz, 2008: 204.

SYSTEMIC FINANCIAL RISKS
AND HOW TO COPE WITH THEM

BY GRAHAME THOMPSON

ACCORDING TO MICHAEL WOODFORD (2009) modern macroeconomics has seen a convergence of views centred around the 'efficient market hypothesis' (EMH). This theoretical position posits that all unfettered markets clear continuously thereby making disequilibria, such as bubbles and crises, highly unlikely. Indeed, in terms of the EMH framework, economic policy designed to eliminate bubbles would lead to 'financial repression': resulting in higher interests rates, the unnecessary rationing of credit and the loss of profitable investment opportunities. That such views about a cosy consensus could have been announced just as the deepest meltdown in financial activity since the 1930s was maturing is perhaps testament to the complacency of conventional economic analysis. But it has not shaken the conventional belief in the virtues of such a framework amongst the mainstream macroeconomic modelling community. Rather the crisis has been interpreted as a simple 'random error' within a still robust EMH framework for economic analysis (Minford 2009). On the other hand the crisis has had some impact on the regulatory and policy making community, as will be discussed in a moment.

One of the key features of this EMH framework in its view of the underlying systemic stability of the economy as a whole is that this leaves little room for the separate consideration of the operational stability of the financial system. Once systemic macroeconomic stability is secured this also provides the necessary conditions for systemic financial stability: these two levels are fused together. But in the wake of the 2007-09 crisis an earlier position has come to challenge this view, namely that associated with Hyman Minsky's 'financial instability thesis' (Minsky 1982, 1986). Minsky's argument was that the more stable the macroeconomic conditions, the more *unstable* becomes the financial system: systemic macroeconomic stability breeds systemic financial instability. This is because as the macro economy seems to stabilize and present continuous growth prospects (the 'long moderation' of 1995-2007) financial players in particular are encouraged to take on more and more risks, which precisely destabilizes the financial system and then the general economy beyond. It lulls financial players into a false sense of security. And this is precisely what seems to have happened in the run up to the 2007-08 financial crisis.

The lessons from this episode are two-fold: first, macroeconomic and financial systems need to be separated out but considered along-side each other in terms of their stability properties; and second, that there is a problem of the systemic risks that continue to pervade just the financial system. *Systemic risk* is associated with the way the entire financial system is interlinked or interdependent so that a problem in respect to a single financial institution (or small cluster of institutions) can cause a cascading and paralysing failure across the whole system. Whilst single markets or instatutions may be exposed to *systematic* risk, this can be mitigated by diversifying into a portfolio so as to minimise this on an individual basis. But systemic risk poses the issue of interdependencies across markets which cannot be tackled simply by aggregating individual exposure to market risks. There are several approaches to deal with this, all of which have received a renewed interest in the post crisis period (deBrandt & Hartman 2000). And this is a very current research agenda for both domestic and international regulatory authorities.

In the international arena the gradual replacement of the Basel II regulatory requirements by a new Basel III system represents the leading edge of this change in emphasis. The Bank of International Settlements (BIS) is charged with regulating the big international banks, and under its pre-crisis Basel II system this concentrated on prudential capital requirement for *individual* banks, which were left more or less to themselves to assess the extent of this as they were charged with implementing their own internal risk assessment models, providing them with an incentive to minimize prudential equity capital held in their account books, so as to maximise the profitable use of thereby freed resources. As a result systemic banking risks escalated. The new Basel III system is designed to address this by concentrating on the *interrelationship* between bank risks ('stress testing' at the systemic level) and by beefing up necessary capital adequacy ratios accordingly (Fender & McGuire 2010). Whether this initiative is enough to prevent further systemic banking collapse remains suspect (Orléan 2010): the capital requirements still look to be minimal and the system is not to be fully implemented until 2019.

A second approach is to concentrate upon modelling 'contagion' between one financial market and another, or between one market in one economy and that in another (Dungey 2008). Contagion represents the extent of externalities or spill-overs between such markets and in principle can estimate the likely systemic impact of a disturbance emerging in a single market on the system of interrelated markets as a whole. This approach involves operationalizing the covariance between 'values at risk' (coVaR) across markets and institutions.

A final overarching approach—which to some extent provides an encompassing framework for all these other initiatives—is to set the financial system within a different paradigmatic universe: to view it as akin to a network operating in the context of an ecological system (Haldane 2009). Systemic risks are modelled, as a result, in a 'non-rationalistic' and 'non-mechanical' operational framework involving complex adaptive feedback mechanisms displaying non-linear reflexive network properties. Whether this can ever be successfully or fully operationalized, or provide the necessary stabilizing regulatory outcome conditions, remains at issue. By and large it still represents a 'top-down' process driven by an all encompassing calculative logic eminating from a single calculative centre. It rather proposes another technical fix for what is at heart a problem of the mobilization and adaptation of 'bottom up' distributed initiatives arising from a series of centres the branching together of which requires continual political mobilization and attention. ☐

GRAHAME THOMPSON *is at Open University and Copenhagen Business School.*

PHOTOGRAPH BY WLADYSLAW SOIKA

THE TOWER
Bank for International Settlements in Basel, Switzerland.

REFERENCES

Allen, B. (1997). "The Logistics Revolution and Transportation." *Annals of the American Academy of Political and Social Science*, 553: 106-116.

Altman, E. I. (1968). "Financial Ratios, Discriminant Analysis and the Prediction of Corporate Bankruptcy," *The Journal of Finance* 23.4.

Amoore , L. and De Goede, M. (2008). *Risk and the War on Terror*. New York and London: Routledge.

Ballou, R.N. (2006). "The Evolution and Future of Logistics and Supply Chain Management." *Produção*, (16) 3: 375-386.

Beck, U. (1992). *Risk society: towards a new modernity*. New York: Sage.

Beck, U. (1999). World risk society. London: Polity.

Beck, U. (2002). "The terrorist threat: world risk society revisited." *Theory, Culture and Society*, 19, 39-55.

Bergsten, F. (2006). "The Peter G. Peterson Institute for International Economics at Twenty Five." Electronic Resource, available at: http://www.iie.com/institute/25anniversary.pdf (accessed 4 April 2011).

Bergsten, F. and W. R. Cline. (1976). "Increasing International Economic Interdependence: The Implications for Research." *The American Economic Review* 66(2): 155-61.

Blackmore, J. M. and R. A. J. Plant. (2008). "Risk and Resilience to Enhance Sustainability with Application to Urban Water Systems." *Journal of Water Resources Planning and Management* 134:224.

Blinder, A. S. et. al. (2001). "How Do Central Banks Talk?" *Geneva Report on the World Economy*, 3. Geneva: International Center for Monetary and Banking Studies.

Bougen, P. D. (2009). "Governing alongside the specter of risk society: legislating US terrorism risk insurance, 2001-2007." *The Open Law Journal*, (2), 33-41.

Bowersox, D.J. (1969). "Physical Distribution Development, Current Status, and Potential." *The Journal of Marketing* 33(1):63-70.

Brown-Waite, G. (2007). "Policy options for extending the terrorism risk insurance act." Electronic resource available at http://www.house.gov/apps/list/hearing/financialsvcs-dem/04-24-07-_policy_proposals_for tria.pdf (Accessed 15 April 2011).

Bruneau, M. et al. (2003). "A Framework to Quantitatively Assess and Enhance the Seismic Resilience of Communities." *Earthquake Spectra* 19:733-752.

Callon, M. (2007). "Performative Economics." In *Do Economists Make Markets?* D. MacKenzie, F. Muniesa, and L. Siu, eds., Princeton: Princeton University Press, p. 311–357.

Cline, W. R. (1969). "Economic Considerations for a Land Reform in Brazil." Ph.D. Dissertation, Yale University.

Cline, W. R. (1982). "External Debt: System Vulnerability and Development." *Columbia Journal of World Business* 17.

Cline, W. R. (1984). *International Debt: Systemic Risk and Policy Response*. Washington, DC Institute for International Economics.

Collier, S. J. and A. Lakoff. (2007). "On Vital Systems Security." Berkeley, CA: Electronic Resource available at http://www.gpia.info/files/u16/Collier_and_Lakoff_2009-01.pdf (Accessed 15 April, 2011).

Collier, S. J. and A. Lakoff. (2008). "The Vulnerability of Vital Systems: How 'Critical Infrastructure' Became a Security Problem." in *The Politics of Securing the Homeland: Critical Infrastructure, Risk and Securitisation*, ed. M. Dunn and K. Kristensen. London and New York: Routledge.

Congressional Research Service (CRS). (2002). *The Economic Effects of 9/11: A Retrospective Assessment*. Available at http://www.fas.org/irp/crs/RL31617.pdf

Congressional Research Service (CRS). (2005). *Border and transportation security: The complexity of the challenge*. Available at <http://www.fas.org/sgp/crs/homesec/RL32839.pdf> (Accessed 29 March, 2007).

Cooper, M. (2006). "Preempting Emergence: The Biological Turn in the War on Terror." *Theory, Culture & Society*, 23(4): 113-135.

Cowen, Deborah (2010) "A Geography of Logistics: Market Authority and the Security of Supply Chains." *The Annals for the Association of American Geographers*, 100(3): 1-21.

Cutter, S. L. et al. (2008). "A Place-Based Model for Understanding Community Resilience to Natural Disasters." *Global Environmental Change* 18:598-606.

deBrandt, O. & Hartman, P. (2000). "Systemic Risk: a Survey," European Central Bank Working Paper No.35, November.

Delanda, M. (1991). *War in the age of intelligent machines*. New York: Zone Books.

Deleuze, G. & Guattari, F. (1987). *A thousand plateaus: capitalism and schizophrenia*. Minneapolis: University of Minnesota Press.

Department of Homeland Security. (2010). "Social Network Analysis for Building Resilient Communities," DHS Solicitation Number BAA10-15, available at http://www.fbo.gov.

Drucker, P. (1962). "The Economy's Dark Continent." *Fortune*, 103-4.

Dungey, M. (2008). "The tsunami: measures of contagion in the 2007-2008 credit crunch" CESifo Forum 4/2008, p. 33-42.

Eisenberg, T. et al. (1989). "The Cornell commission: on Morris and the worm." *Communications of the ACM* 32:706-709. http://portal.acm.org/citation.cfm?doid=63526.63530.

Ellis, J. et al. (1997). "Report to the President's Commission on Critical Infrastructure Protection." http://citeseerx.ist.psu.edu/viewdoc/summary?doi=10.1.1.57.2240.

Fender, I. & McGuire, P. (2010) "Bank structure, funding risk and the transmission of shocks across countries: concepts and measurement." *BIS Quarterly Review*, September, pp. 63-79.

Fisher, G.H. (1956). "Weapon System Cost Analysis." *Operations Research*, 56 (4): 558-571.

Flynn, S. 2(003). "The False Conundrum: Continental Integration versus Homeland Security." In *Rebordering North America*, ed. P.

Andreas and T.J. Biersteker. New York: Routledge, p. 110-127.

Folke, C. (2006). "Resilience: The Emergence of a Perspective for Social–Ecological Systems Analyses." *Global Environmental Change* 16:253-267.

Foucault, M. (1991). "On governmentality," in G. Burchell, C. Gordon and P. Miller,(eds), *The Foucault effect: studies in governmentality.* Hemel Hempstead: Harvester Wheatsheaf.

Frank, C. R., and W. R. Cline (1971). "Measurement of Debt Servicing Capacity: An Application of Discriminant Analysis." *Journal of International Economics* 1: 327-44.

Frank, C.R., and W. R. Cline. (1969). "Debt Servicing and Foreign Assistance: An Analysis of Problems and Prospects in Less Developed Countries." Office of Program and Policy Coordination: US AID.

Galison, P. (1994). "Ontology of the Enemy: Norbert Wiener and the Cybernetic Vision." *Critical Inquiry*, 21 (1):228-266.

Globerman, S. and Storer, R. (2009). "The Effects of 9/11 on Canadian-U.S. Trade: An Update through 2008." Brookings Institute. Available at http://www.brookings.edu/papers/2009/0713_canada_globerman.aspx

Greenspan, A. (2005) "Economic Flexibility." In The National Association for Business Economics Annual Meeting. Chicago, Illinois.

Gunderson, L. H. (2000). "Ecological Resilience - In Theory and Application." *Annual Review of Ecology and Systematics* 31:425-439.

Haldane, A. (2009). "Rethinking the financial network." Bank of England electronic resource available at: http://www.bankofengland.co.uk/publications/speeches/2009/speech386.pdf

Haveman, J.D. and H.J. Shatz. (2006). *Protecting the nation's seaports: balancing security and cost.* San Francisco: Public Policy Institute of California.

Heims, S. (1991). *The Cybernetics Group.* Cambridge: MIT Press.

Holling, C. S. (1973). "Resilience and Stability of Ecological Systems." *Annual Review of Ecology and Systematics* 4:1-23.

Holling, C. S. (1996). "Engineering Resilience versus Ecological Resilience." Pp. 31-44 in *Engineering within Ecological Constraints.* National Academies Press.

Holling, C.S. (1966). "Building Models of Complex Systems." In K.E.F. Watt (Ed.), *Systems Analysis in Ecology* (pp. 195-214). New York: Academic Press.

Holmes, D. R. (2009). "Economy of words," *Cultural Anthropology.* 24:381-419.

House Committee on Government Operations (1956) *Civil Defense for National Survival.* Washington, DC: US Government Printing Office.

Hutchinson G.E. (1948). "Circular Causal Systems in Ecology." *Annals of the New York Academy of Science*, 40:221-246.

Joint Committee on Defense Production. (1958). Seventh Annual Report of the Activities of the Joint Committee on Defense Production. January 16. Washington: US Government Printing Office.

Jomini, B. (2009 [1836]). *The Art of War.* Kingston, ON: Legacy Books Press Classics.

Keynes, J. M. (2007 [1936]). *The General Theory of Employment, Interest and Money.* The Royal Economic Society. Basingstoke, UK: Palgrave.

Kingsland, S.E. (1995). *Modeling Nature: Episodes in the History of Population Ecology.* Chicago: Universityof Chicago Press.

Knight, F.H. (1921). *Risk, Uncertainty, and Profit.* Boston, MA: Houghton Mifflin Company.

Lakoff, G. and M. Johnson (1980). *The Metaphors We Live By.* Chicago: University of Chicago Press.

Lalonde, B. (1994). "Perspectives on Logistics Management." In *The Logistics Handbook.* Robeson, J.F. and Copacino, W. C., (eds) New York: The Free Press.

Lalonde, B., Grabner, J., and Robeson, J. (1970). "Integrated Distribution Management: A management Perspective." *International Journal of Physical Distribution.* October 1st.

LeKashman, R. and Stolle, J.F. (1965) "The Total Cost Approach to Distribution." *Business Horizons.* Winter: 33-46.

Logistics Management Institute (LMI). (n.d.). *LMI history.* http://www.lmi.org/aboutus/History.aspx (last accessed 20 August 2010).

Lovins, A. and L. H. Lovins. (2001). *Brittle Power: Energy Strategy for National Security.* Andover, MA: Brickhouse Publishing. (Original work published in 1982).

MacKenzie, D. (2001). "Physics and Finance: S-Terms and Modern Finance as a Topic for Science Studies." *Science, Technology and Human Values* 26(2):115–144.

MacKenzie, D. (2006). *An Engine, Not a Camera: How Financial Models Shape Markets.* Cambridge, MA: MIT Press.

MacKenzie, D. F. Muniesa, and L. Siu (2006). "Introduction." In *Do Economists Make Markets?* D. MacKenzie, F. Muniesa, and L. Siu, eds. Princeton: Princeton University Press, p. 1–19.

Madni, A. M., and S. Jackson. (2009). "Towards a Conceptual Framework for Resilience Engineering." *IEEE Systems Journal* 3:181-191.

Magee, J.F. (1960). "The Logistics of Distribution." *Harvard Business Review*, 40: 89-101.

McCloskey, D. (1985). *The Rhetoric of Economics.* Madison: University of Wisconsin Press.

McCloskey, D. (1994). *Knowledge and Persuasion in Economics.* Cambridge: Cambridge University Press.

McCloskey, D., (1990). *If You're So Smart: The Narrative of Economic Expertise.* Chicago: University of Chicago Press.

McIntosh, R. (1988). *The Background of Ecology: Concept and Theory.* Cambridge: University of Cambridge.

Military Operations Subcommittee of the House Committee on Government Operations (1956). *Civil Defense for National Survival.* Washington, DC: Government Printing Office, p. 1080.

Minford, P. (2009) "The banking crisis – a rational interpretation," Cardiff Business School Economics Working Papers, E2009/10, July.

Minsky, H. P. (1982), *Can "It" Happen Again: Essays on Instability and Finance,* Armonk: M.E. Sharpe.

Minsky, H. P. (1986), *Stabilizing an Unstable Economy,* New Haven: Yale University Press.

Mitchell, T. (2009). "Carbon Democracy," *Economy and Society*, 38(3):399 – 432.

Napolitano, J. (2010). "A New Framework for Security: Remarks as Prepared by Secretary Napolitano to New York City First Responders," September 10 (Available at: http://www.dhs.gov/ynews/speeches/sp_1284133372649.shtm).

Nelson, S. and P. Katzenstein (n.d.). "Uncertainty and Risk and the Crisis of 2008." Unpublished ms.

Norris, F. H.,et.al. (2008). "Community Resilience as a Metaphor, Theory, Set of Capacities, and Strategy for Disaster Readiness." American Journal of *Community Psychology* 41:127-150.

Orléan, A. (2010) "The impossible evaluation of risk" *Prisme* No.18, April: Cournot Centre for Economic Studies, Paris.

Ozgöde, O. (2008). "Logistics of National Survival," Department of Sociology, Columbia University, 2008.

Palladino, P. (1991). "Defining Ecology: Ecological Theories, Mathematical Models, and Applied Biology in the 1960s and 1970s." *Journal of the History of Biology*, 24 (2, Summer): 223-243.

Patten, B. (1966). "Systems Ecology: A Course Sequence in Mathematical Ecology." *BioScience*, 16 (9, Sept.): 593-598.

Pettit, T.J., Fiksel, J. and Croxton, K.L. (2010). "Ensuring Supply Chain Resilience: Development of a Conceptual Framework. *Journal of Business Logistics*, (31)1: 1-21.

Reifer, T. (2004). "Labor, Race & Empire: Transport Workers & Transnational Empires of Trade, Production, and Finance." In *Labor Versus Empire: Race, Gender, and Migration*, ed. G. Gonzalez & R. Fernandez. Routledge: London and New York, p. 17-36.

Rice, J. and Caniato, F. (2003). "Supply Chain Response to Terrorism: Creating Resilient and Secure Supply Chains." MIT Center for Transportation and Logistics. Supply Chain Response to Terrorism Project, Interim Report of Progress and Learnings, August 8. Available online at: http://web.mit.edu/scresponse/repository/SC_Resp_Report_Interim_Final_8803.pdf

Richter, P.H. & Peitgen, H.O. (1985). "Morphology of complex boundaries." *Berichte der Bundesgesellschaft fur Physikalische Chemie*, 89:571-578.

Riles, A. (2001). "Real-Time: Governing the Market After the Failure of Knowledge." Paper presented at the University of California at Berkeley, Department of Anthropology, January 18.

Riles, A. (2004). "Real Time: Unwinding Technocratic and Anthropological Knowledge." *American Ethnologist* 31(3):392–405.

Riles, A. (2010) *Collateral Knowledge: Legal Reason in Global Financial Markets.* Chicago: University of Chicago Press.

Rinaldi, S.M., J.P. Peerenboom, and T.K. Kelly. (2001). "Identifying, understanding, and analyzing critical infrastructure interdependencies." *IEEE Control Systems Magazine* 21:11-25.

Samuelson, P. (1947) *Foundations of Economic Analysis.* Cambridge, MA: Harvard University Press.

Schwarcz, Daniel (2008). "Redesigning Consumer Dispute Resolution: A Case Study of the British and American Approaches to Insurance Claims Conflict " *Tulane Law Review* 83:735.

Skidelsky, R. (1992) *John Maynard Keynes, vol. 2: The Economist as Savior 1920–1937*. New York: Penguin.

Smart, G. (1999). "Storytelling in a Central Bank: The Role of Narrative in the Creation and Use of Economic Knowledge." *Journal of Business and Technical Communication* 13:249–273.

Smart, G. (2006). *Writing the Economy: Activity, Genre and Technology in the World of Banking.* London: Equinox.

Smykay, E. W. and B.J. LaLonde. (1967). *Physical Distribution: The New and Profitable Science of Business Logistics.* Chicago, London: Dartnell Press.

Spafford, E. H. (1989). "Crisis and aftermath." *Communications of the ACM* 32:678. http://portal.acm.org/citation.cfm?id=63527

Star, S. L., and J. Griesemer. (1989). "Institutional Ecology, 'Translations' and Boundary Objects: Amateurs and Professionals in Berkeley's Museum of Vertebrate Zoology, 1907-1939." *Social Studies of Science* 19:387-420.

Subcommittee on Telecommunications and Finance of the Committee on Energy and Commerce. (1994) Testimony by Alan Greenspan, Chairman, Board of Governors of the Federal Reserve System, May 25.

Summers, L. (1991). "The scientific illusion in empirical macroeconomics," *Scandinavian Journal of Economics*, 93(2):129-148.

Taylor, P. (1988). "Technocratic Optimism, HT Odum and the Partial Transformation of the Ecological Metaphor after World War II." *Journal of the History of Biology*, 21: 213-244.

Thayer, S. B. and W. W. Shaner, (1960). "Effects of Nuclear Attacks on the Petroleum Industry." Stanford, California: Stanford Research Institute.

von Neumann, J. and O. Morgenstern (1947). *The Theory of Games and Economic Behavior,* Princeton, N.J.: Princeton University Press, 2nd edition.

Watt, K. (1962). "Use of mathematics in population ecology." *Annual Review of Entomology*, 7: 243–260.

Watt, K. (1966a). "The Nature of Systems Analysis." In K. Watt (Ed.) *Systems Analysis in Ecology*. New York: Academic Press.

Watt, K. (1966b). "Ecology in the Future." In K. Watt (Ed.) *Systems Analysis in Ecology*. New York: Academic Press.

Watts, D J, and S. H. Strogatz. (1998). "Collective dynamics of 'small-world' networks." *Nature* 393:440-2.

Weaver, N., V. Paxson, S. Staniford, and R. Cunningham. (2003). "A Taxonomy of Computer Worms." *Proceeedings of WORM'03*. Washington, DC, p. 11-18.

Wilbanks, T. J. (2010). "Remarks at workshop session 'Resilience? What's That?'" Natural Hazards Research and Applications Workshop, Broomfield, CO, July 9-12.

Wildavsky, A. (1966). "The Political Economy of Efficiency: Cost-Benefit Analysis, Systems Analysis, and Program Budgeting." *Public Administration Review*, (26) 4: 292-310.

Williamson, J. (1990). "What Washington Means by Policy Reform." In *Latin American Adjustment : How Much Has Happened?* edited by John Williamson, xv, 445 p. Washington, D.C.: Institute for International Economics.

Williamson, J., and Institute for International Economics (U.S.). (1990) *Latin American Adjustment : How Much Has Happened?* Washington, D.C.: Institute for International Economics.

Woodford, M. (2009) "Convergence in macroeconomics: elements of the new synthesis," *American Economic Journal of Macroeconomics*, Vol.1, No.1, pp.267-79.

Zaloom, Caitlin (2003) "Ambiguous Numbers: Trading Technologies and Interpretation in Financial Markets." *American Ethnologist* 30:258–272.

Limn is published as needed. This issue is set using the typefaces Minion Pro and Graphik. **Design**: Martin Hoyem/American Ethnography. **Über-Editorial Bureau**: Stephen J. Collier, Christopher M. Kelty, and Andrew Lakoff. **Issue No. 1 Editors**: Stephen J. Collier, Christopher M. Kelty, and Andrew Lakoff **||** This magazine Copyright © 2011 Stephen Collier, Christopher Kelty, Andrew Lakoff and Martin Hoyem. All articles herein are Copyright © 2011 by their respective authors. This magazine may not be reproduced without permission, however the articles are available online at http://limn.it/ and available for unrestricted use under a Creative Commons 3.0 unported License, http://creativecommons.org/licenses/by-sa/3.0/ **||** Publication assistance provided by the Center for Society and Genetics, University of California, Los Angeles; University of Southern California and The New School, New York.

More at http://limn.it/